brilliant

Microsoft®
Excel
2007

POCKET BOOK

J. Peter Bruzzese

PEARSON
Prentice
Hall

Harlow, England • London • New York • Boston • San Francisco • Toronto • Sydney • Singapore • Hong Kong
Tokyo • Seoul • Taipei • New Delhi • Cape Town • Madrid • Mexico City • Amsterdam • Munich • Paris • Milan

Pearson Education Limited
Edinburgh Gate
Harlow CM20 2JE
Tel: +44 (0) 1279 623623
Fax: +44 (0) 1279 431059
Website: www.pearsoned.co.uk

First published in Great Britain in 2007

© Joli Ballew 2007

The right of J. Peter Bruzzese to be identified as author of this work has been asserted
by him in accordance with the Copyright, Designs and Patents Act 1988.

ISBN: 978-0-132-05922-0

British Library Cataloguing-in-Publication Data
A catalogue record for this book is available from the British Library

10 9 8 7 6 5 4 3 2 1
11 10 09 08 07

Typeset in 10pt Helvetica Roman by 30
Printed and bound in Great Britain by Ashford Colour Press, Gosport

The Publisher's policy is to use paper manufactured from sustainable forests.

Brilliant Pocket Books

What you need to know – when you need it!

When you're working on your PC and come up against a problem that you're unsure how to solve, or want to accomplish something in an application that you aren't sure how to do, where do you look? If you are fed up with wading through pages of background information in unwieldy manuals and training guides trying to find the piece of information or advice that you need RIGHT NOW, and if you find helplines really aren't that helpful, then Brilliant Pocket Books are the answer!

Brilliant Pocket Books have been developed to allow you to find the info that you need easily and without fuss and to guide you through each task using a highly visual step-by-step approach – providing exactly what you need to know, when you need it!

Brilliant Pocket Books are concise, easy-to-access guides to all of the most common important and useful tasks in all of the applications in the Office 2007 suite. Short, concise lessons make it really easy to learn any particular feature, or master any task or problem that you will come across in day-to-day use of the applications.

When you are faced with any task on your PC, whether major or minor, that you are unsure about, your Brilliant Pocket Book will provide you with the answer – almost before you know what the question is!

Brilliant Pocket Books Series

Series Editor: Joli Ballew

Brilliant Microsoft® Access 2007 Pocket Book *S.E.Slack*

Brilliant Microsoft® Excel 2007 Pocket Book *J. Peter Bruzzese*

Brilliant Microsoft® Office 2007 Pocket Book *Jerri Ledford & Rebecca Freshour*

Brilliant Microsoft® Outlook 2007 Pocket Book *Meryl K. Evans*

Brilliant Microsoft® PowerPoint 2007 Pocket Book *S. E. Slack*

Brilliant Microsoft® Windows Vista 2007 Pocket Book *Jerri Ledford & Rebecca Freshour*

Brilliant Microsoft® Word 2007 Pocket Book *Deanna Reynolds*

Contents

Introduction

Welcome to the *Brilliant Microsoft® Excel Pocket Book* – a handy visual quick reference that will give you a basic grounding in the common features and tasks that you will need to master to use Microsoft® Excel 2007 in any day-to-day situation. Keep it on your desk, in your briefcase or bag – or even in your pocket! – and you will always have the answer to hand for any problem or task that you come across.

Find out what you need to know – when you need it!

You don't have to read this book in any particular order. It is designed so that you can jump in, get the information you need and jump out – just look up the task in the contents list, turn to the right page, read the introduction, follow the step-by-step instructions – and you're done!

How this book works

Each section in this book includes foolproof step-by-step instructions for performing specific tasks, using screenshots to illustrate each step. Additional information is included to help increase your understanding and develop your skills – these are identified by the following icons:

 Jargon buster – New or unfamiliar terms are defined and explained in plain English to help you as you work through a section.

 Timesaver tip – These tips give you ideas that cut corners and confusion. They also give you additional information related to the topic that you are currently learning. Use them to expand your knowledge of a particular feature or concept.

 Important – This identifies areas where new users often run into trouble, and offers practical hints and solutions to these problems.

Brilliant Pocket Books **are a handy, accessible resource that you will find yourself turning to time and time again when you are faced with a problem or an unfamiliar task and need an answer at your fingertips – or in your pocket!**

1

Getting Started with Excel 2007

In this lesson you will learn how to manoeuvre through the new Excel 2007 ribbon interface. You will also learn how to customise your working environment and increase your productivity through shortcut keys. Finally, you will begin working with Excel 2007 workbooks and worksheets, everything from creating a workbook and renaming worksheets, to saving those documents as Excel files or even PDFs!

→ Getting Familiar with the Excel 2007 Interface

The first Windows version of Excel was released in 1987. And now, Excel 2007 is the latest version of Microsoft's sophisticated spreadsheet application. Its purpose, that of creating workbooks to handle the analysis of numerical data through formula calculations and graphical charting, has remained unchanged, although the interface and extent of its capabilities have improved consistently over the years. Excel 2007 boasts powerful improvements from previous versions, as well as a new **ribbon** interface to make it easier to access the tools you need, as you can see in Figure 1.1.

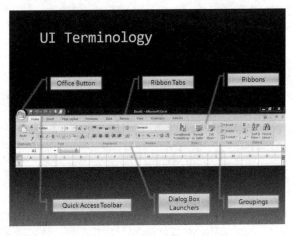

Figure 1.1
The new Excel 2007 user interface.

The new user interface (UI) includes the following features:

■ *The Office Button*: This circular launching pad in the upper left-hand corner of your application allows you to open new or existing documents, save or print these documents, prepare a document for distribution, or configure special application options.

■ *Ribbons*: These have groupings of tools to make it easier to find the command option you need. Each ribbon has a named tab (for example, the Home ribbon has a tab that says **Home**). Not all ribbons will appear by default. Some are contextual ribbons in that they appear only when you perform an action that causes them to appear.

Jargon buster

Contextual ribbons appear only as a result of a specific action on your part. For example, if you create a table or add a picture, you will see additional ribbons that allow you to format those items.

■ *Groupings*: Each ribbon has a set of tools arranged into groups (or groupings). For example, on the Insert ribbon you see the grouping **Charts** which includes a prearranged selection of charting types.

■ *Dialog Box Launchers*: In the bottom right-hand corner of some of your groupings you will notice a little arrow that will open an additional dialogue that relates to the grouping it is connected to.

■ *Galleries*: These show you "live previews" of your formatting styles by hovering over an option before you actually make your selection. The gallery will show you what *might* be the result with your formatting choice, but live previews show you what *will* be by altering the actual objects within the document to make it easier for you to choose.

Important

In previous versions of Excel we had menus and toolbars that you could configure by adding or removing toolbar buttons and commands. However, in Excel 2007 the ribbon settings are able to be changed only by a programmer who has XML coding experience and the information freely provided by Microsoft at the Office Developer Center (**http://msdn.microsoft.com/office/**).

→ Customise the Excel 2007 Interface: Quick Access Toolbar

You cannot change the ribbons; however, you can alter the Quick Access Toolbar located next to your Office Button.

Jargon buster

Quick Access Toolbar allows you to place all your favourite command buttons in one easy-to-access location. These can be commands that do not currently reside on a ribbon, or even those commands that you use often, although they have a ribbon placement.

To alter the location of the Quick Access Toolbar or the display of your ribbons, perform one of the following:

1 Select the down arrow next to your Quick Access Toolbar and choose the option **Show Below the Ribbon** to move the toolbar underneath the ribbons.

2 Select the **Minimize the Ribbon** option to increase your desktop work space while allowing only the ribbon tabs to show. You can select a tab and see the corresponding ribbon and it will disappear when you have finished working with it.

3 Select from the list of preconfigured buttons (i.e. Undo, Redo and so forth) to quickly add important functionality.

4 Select the **More Commands...** option to search for and add other command options that aren't readily available (shown in Figure 1.2).

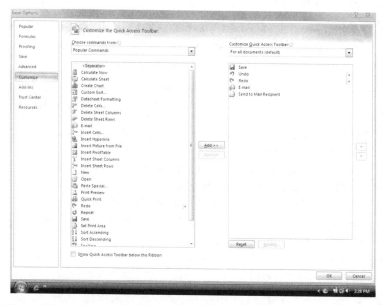

Figure 1.2
Adding Command buttons to your Quick Access Toolbar.

If you choose **More Commands...** then you will need to do   the following to add more command options to your Quick Access Toolbar:

1 From the section **Choose commands from** you can select the down arrow and choose from specific ribbons or contextual ribbons that you wish to duplicate a command from. You can also select from several embracive options such as **Commands Not In The Ribbon**.

2 Once you find the button you are looking for, select it and choose **Add>>** to include it with your Quick Access Toolbar.

3 From the **Customize Quick Access Toolbar** settings you can decide whether you want this change made on all Quick Access Toolbars you use from Excel or just this particular workbook.

4 Use the up and down arrows on the right side of the dialogue box to alter the location of the button within the Quick Access Toolbar.

5 When you have finished, you can select OK. If you are unsure, you can choose the **Reset** button and start all over again.

Important

Too often people get comfortable with their applications before making the neccessary adjustments for them to work well for them. Like an office chair – you sit down, forget to adjust it and sit awkwardly for the next 10 years. Don't allow this to happen with Excel (or any of the other Office applications). You must take advantage of the ability to configure your Quick Access Toolbar as it is one of the configuration adjustments you have at your disposal.

→ Using Shortcut Keys in Excel 2007

So you want to be a maverick who never uses a mouse? There are literally hundreds of shortcut keys you can memorise for Excel 2007. For a list of useful shortcuts you can view the Excel developers' blog site at **http://blogs.msdn.com/excel/archive/2006/02/23/538311.aspx**

However, you can easily find useful shortcut keys by hitting the **Alt** key. When you hit the **Alt** key your shortcuts will appear throughout your interface.

For example, to add a new worksheet using shortcut keys and the **Alt** command, you do the following:

1 Select the **Alt** button.

2 Select Alt+H (to bring up Home ribbon shortcuts).

3 Select Alt+I (for Insert shortcuts).

4 Select Alt+S (to insert the new worksheet).

Timesaver tip

Using the Alt key is a great way to work with Excel 2007 shortcuts, but not the fastest. For example, to insert a new worksheet in a faster way you would hold down Shift+Alt and press F1. For a .pdf chart of other shortcuts go to **http://isamrad.com/dgainer/1_02-23-2006.pdf**

→ Working with Workbooks

The starting point for any Excel document is the workbook, which initially contains three worksheets.

Jargon buster

Excel worksheets are spreadsheets that are made up of cells organised into columns and rows. Worksheets allow you to organise, manipulate and analyse your data. Excel 2007 allows you to have over 1 million rows and 16,000 columns (over 16 billion cells for your data), so you don't have to worry about not having enough room in your spreadsheet.

Start a New Workbook

When you open Excel it will automatically create a workbook named Book1. This workbook is based on a template file called book.xlt, which is used to create all default workbooks. If you open the template file and make any change to it (for example, adding more worksheets), then all future documents created off that template will have the changes.

To begin a new workbook, follow these steps:

1 Select your Office Button using your mouse.

2 Select **New** (shown in Figure 1.3).

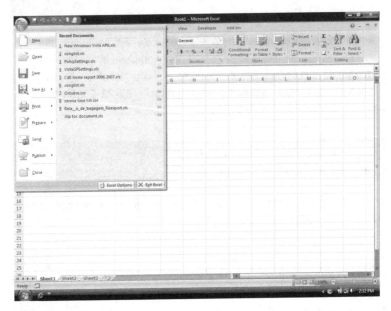

Figure 1.3
Starting a new workbook.

3 Make sure you have **Blank and recent** as the setting of your templates.

4 Then choose **Blank Workbook** and select **Create** (shown in Figure 1.4).

Timesaver tip

You could create a new workbook by selecting Ctrl+N.

Figure 1.4
Create a new workbook from the default template.

Open an Existing Workbook

You may have a workbook already that you work on, or one that someone else has given you to work with.

To open an existing workbook, follow these steps:

1 Select your Office Button using your mouse.

2 Select **Open** and look in the current folder for the document you are wanting to open. If it isn't there, navigate to the folder you need (or perform a search for the file if you know its name) until you find it.

3 If you want to see a preview of your workbook first, you may have to alter the pane you are looking at. Select the Organize button, hover your mouse over the Layout options and select the Preview Pane (which will show you the document preview in a side window).

4 Select the workbook and choose **Open**.

Saving and Naming Your Workbooks

After adding your data into various cells in your worksheets you need to make sure you don't lose that data. You not only want to save your workbook but name it in such a way that it is easy for you to find it again later.

To save your workbook, follow these steps:

1 Select your Office Button using your mouse.

2 Select **Save**.

3 Choose a location and select the **Save** button.

Saving Your Workbook under a Different Name or File Format

You may open up a workbook and decide you want to keep the current workbook as it is but use it as the basis for a new document. You can therefore save the workbook under a different name.

To save your workbook under a different name, follow these steps.

1 Select your Office Button using your mouse.

2 Place your cursor over **Save As** and your options will expand (as shown in Figure 1.5).

3 Choose **Excel Workbook**.

4 Choose a location and select the **Save** button.

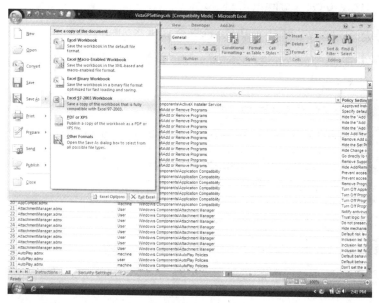

Figure 1.5
Save As options for your documents.

You may also want to save your documents in different file formats. Excel 2007 supports many file formats – you can research these in the Excel Help files by selecting the little blue question mark in the upper right-hand corner of your Excel UI and typing in **File formats that are supported in Excel**.

However, there are three you should be aware of for now:

- *.xlsx*: The default file format for Excel 2007, which saves documents in an XML format.

- *.xltx*: Saves documents as templates for Excel 2007.

- *.xls*: The file format used for backward compatibility with Excel applications from 1997–2003.

If you need to save an Excel 2007 .xlsx document into another format, let's say one for backward compatibility, you can do this in two ways.

First, you can perform the following:

1 Select your Office Button using your mouse.

2 Place your cursor over **Save As** and your options will expand.

3 Choose **Excel Workbook**.

4 From the **Save as type** options, select the down arrow.

5 Choose the file format you would like.

6 Choose a location and select the **Save** button.

Second, you can perform the following:

1 Select your Office Button using your mouse.

2 Place your cursor over **Save As** and your options will expand.

3 Choose **Excel 97–2003 Workbook**.

4 You'll notice in the **Save as type** options that the .xls format is already selected for you.

5 Choose a location and select the **Save** button.

Saving Your Workbook as a PDF or XPS Document

At times you may need to save your workbooks into a completely different type of format, such as PDF or XPS.

Jargon buster

Portable Document Format (PDF) is a format that preserves the look of your document for sharing while making it un-editable at the same time. Some quality is lost in the conversion process. To read PDF files you need a reader, the most popular being the free Adobe Acrobat Reader.

Jargon buster

XML Paper Specification (XPS) is also a format for sharing documents. With XPS none of the quality is lost in the conversion process. There are free XPS readers available online, although Windows Vista includes one with the OS (Operating System).

To save a document as either PDF or XPS you can perform the following:

1 Select your Office Button using your mouse.

2 Place your cursor over **Save As** and your options will expand.

3 Choose **PDF or XPS**.

4 You'll notice in the **Save as type** options that the .pdf format is selected (as shown in Figure 1.6), but you can choose the down arrow and change it to .xps if you like.

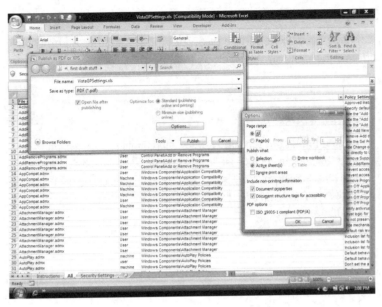

Figure 1.6
Saving a document as PDF or XPS.

5 You can alter the size/quality of the converted document by choosing either:

- Standard (publishing online and printing)

- Minimum size (publishing online).

6 Select the **Options** button to determine which pages are converted within your worksheet and which worksheets you want converted. You can also decide whether you want document properties included with the converted document.

7 Choose a location and select the **Save** button.

→ Working with Worksheets

The starting point for any Excel document is the workbook, which initially contains three worksheets called Sheet1, Sheet2 and Sheet3. You may want to add more worksheets, however, to facilitate organising your data for an extremely complex project. Or you may want to add worksheets to simply keep track of data monthly, which would require one sheet for each month. You can add more sheets easily by doing one of the following:

1 To insert a new worksheet at the end of your existing worksheets you can select the **Insert Worksheet** button at the end of the row of worksheets (or you can press Shift+F11).

2 To insert a new worksheet before a specific worksheet, select the worksheet you want and then, from the Home ribbon, the Cells grouping, select Insert and then Insert Sheet.

3 If you right-click an existing worksheet you are then presented with a list of options. Select **Insert** and then choose **Worksheet** and then OK.

Timesaver tip

To insert multiple sheets at once you can hold down the Shift key and select the sheets you currently have, one at a time, causing them to be highlighted. Once you have selected the number of sheets you need, you go to the Home ribbon, the Cells grouping and choose Insert, then Insert Sheet.

Navigating Worksheets

To go from one worksheet to another you simply have to select the sheet you want. However, sometimes you have so many sheets that you cannot see them all. In the bottom left-hand corner of your interface are four arrows. The first one will take you to the beginning of all your sheets. The second moves you backwards through your sheets one at a time. The third moves you forwards through your sheets one at a time. The fourth moves you to the end of all your sheets.

Timesaver tip

If you right-click any of the four navigation arrows you will be able to see a list of all the worksheets for that workbook. You can select any sheet to navigate immediately to that point.

Rename or Delete a Worksheet

There are often multiple ways to do the same thing in Excel 2007. We will show you two ways to rename or delete a worksheet.

To rename a worksheet, perform one of the following:

1 Right-click the worksheet you wish to rename (as shown in Figure 1.7). Choose Rename and then type in the new name in the Sheet tab.

2 Select the worksheet you wish to rename. From the Home ribbon, the Cells grouping, select the Format option and choose **Rename Sheet**.

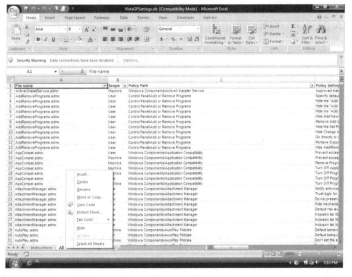

Figure 1.7
Right-click your worksheet to see your options.

Important

When naming your worksheets there are a few rules to keep in mind. First off, you cannot exceed 31 characters. You can, however, use spaces, parentheses and brackets (although brackets cannot be used at the beginning of the name for some reason). You cannot use any of the following characters as part of a sheet name: / \ ? * : (forward slash, backslash, question mark, asterisk, or colon); however commas and exclamation marks are allowed.

To delete a worksheet, perform one of the following:

1 Right-click the worksheet you wish to delete. Choose Delete.

2 Select the worksheet you wish to delete. From the Home ribbon, the Cells grouping, select the Delete option and choose **Delete Sheet**.

Hide a Worksheet

At times you may have data that doesn't need to be changed often, or a worksheet that you do not wish others to see if they open your workbook. You can hide the worksheet. Although this doesn't protect it completely, because a person can unhide it if he/she wants, it does provide a level of security by making it inaccessible and prevents accidental changes to your data.

To hide/unhide a worksheet, perform the following:

1 Select the worksheet you wish to hide.

2 From the Home ribbon, the Cells grouping, select the **Format** option.

3 Under the heading Visibility, hover your mouse over the **Hide & Unhide** setting and then select **Hide Sheet**.

4 To see the hidden sheets in your workbook, go back to the same **Hide & Unhide** options and choose **Unhide Sheet**. You will be shown a list of hidden sheets to choose to make visible.

Move or Copy a Worksheet

To move (or make a copy of) a worksheet with your mouse, perform the following:

1 Select the worksheet you wish to move by clicking and holding down the left mouse button. (Note: If you wish to copy the sheet you select, hold down the Ctrl button as you drag it.)

2 Now drag the sheet along and watch the little black triangle pointer move until you reach the new location. (Note: If you are copying the sheet you will see a little plus sign in the centre of the graphical sheet that appears.)

3 Release the mouse button to complete the move.

To move (or make a copy of) a worksheet with interface options, perform the following:

1 Right-click any of the worksheets and select the **Move or Copy** option. (Note: You can find the same option by looking at the Home ribbon, the Cells grouping, under the Format settings you see **Move or Copy**.)

2 From here you can copy the worksheet to an entirely different workbook, or move the worksheet before another sheet in the lineup (or to the end of the lineup) or make a copy of the worksheet.

Change Your Worksheet Tab Colours

One way to help you organise your worksheets is to go beyond naming and actually give your worksheet tabs different colours. To alter the colour of your worksheet, perform the following:

1 Right-click the worksheet you wish to change, hover your cursor over the **Tab Color** setting and then pick a colour you think will work with that tab. (Note: You can find the same option by looking at the Home ribbon, the Cells grouping, under the Format settings you see the **Tab Color** settings, as shown in Figure 1.8.)

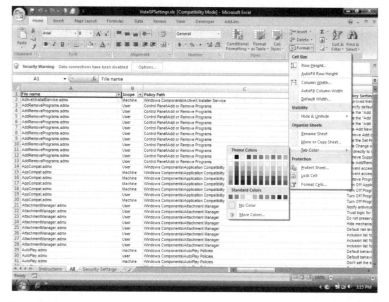

Figure 1.8
Changing Tab Colour settings from the Cells grouping.

2 From here you can colour other worksheets with different colours or just the ones you feel need to stand apart from the others.

It's best not to overdo this option. It can be time consuming to worry about the colour of your tabs. But you may find it helps you distinguish groupings of data or summary sheets.

→ Using Excel Templates

Earlier we discussed creating a new workbook from the standard book.xltx template. There are a few important points you should know about Excel template use:

1 You can use a predefined template from Excel which includes a variety of styles such as Expense Reports, or Personal Monthly Budget, or even a Project To-Do List. To use one of these templates, when you start a new document, under the

Templates pane, choose the **Installed Templates** option (shown in Figure 1.9) and select the template you would like to try. You will see a mini-preview of your template on the right side of your dialogue box.

Figure 1.9
Create a new workbook from a preconfigured template.

2 You can also choose from a variety of online templates that Microsoft provides through the Microsoft Office Online connection. These include scores of templates that will help you do everything from budget to invoices to purchase orders. To use one of these templates, when you start a new document, under the Templates pane (where it says Microsoft Office Online), choose one of the template types. (Note: You must have a working Internet connection for these templates to appear.) You will see a list of options and you can choose to download and try any of these for free.

→ Closing and Exiting Excel

When you have finished working on your Excel workbook, you need to save it and then close it (although if you try to close the document without saving you will be presented with the option to save it first). You learned earlier how to save it.

To close your Excel workbook, perform the following:

1 Select the Office Button and choose **Close**.

2 If you've already saved the document, it will simply close. If not, it will ask whether you want to save the changes you made to the document.

Another way to close your workbook is to select the little x located at the top right-hand corner of your document (not to be mistaken for the X that closes Excel).

Once all workbooks are saved and closed, you can exit Excel. The easy way to do this is simply to select the X located at the top right-hand corner of your application. You could also select the Office Button and choose the **Exit Excel** option.

2

Working with Your Excel Spreadsheet

In this lesson you will learn methods of adding data into your workbooks, including text, comments, numbers, dates and times. You will also learn some tricks on how to navigate more smoothly through your spreadsheets (which can become quite large at times).

→ Entering Data into Your Worksheet

Your Excel spreadsheet is made up of columns and rows. Columns are labelled with letters, rows are labelled with numbers. At the intersection between a column and a row you have cells. Each cell in your spreadsheet has its own unique location made up of the column heading label and the row heading label. For example, A22 would be a cell located in column A, row 22.

Insert Data into Cells

To insert data into a cell, you perform the following:

1 Using your mouse, select the cell you wish to add data into.

2 Type the text (which can include text, numbers, dates, times, formulas and functions).

3 Notice that the data you insert appears in the Formula Bar (shown in Figure 2.1).

4 Press Enter and notice that the text is entered left-aligned by default and your text insertion point moves to the next cell down. Note: You could press Tab to move the cursor to the next cell to the right as well.

Important

If you want to move your insertion point up after entering data, you press Shift+Enter. If you want to move your insertion point to the left after entering data, you press Shift+Tab.

Navigate to a Specific Cell

If you are working with a worksheet that is quite large and would like to navigate directly to a specific cell, you can use the **Name Box** (shown in Figure 2.1) or the **Go To** dialogue box.

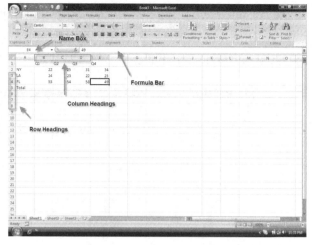

Figure 2.1
Insert data into cells and watch it appear in the formula bar.

To use the Name Box, perform the following:

1 Select the Name Box.

2 Enter a cell reference (D9, for example).

3 Press enter and you jump to that cell.

Timesaver tip

To pick from a list of all named ranges in the current workbook, even on different worksheets within the current workbook, click the down arrow to the right of the Name Box.

To use the Go To dialogue, perform the following:

1 To open the Go To dialogue you can press F5 or Ctrl+G. You could also select the Home ribbon, under the Editing grouping, the Find & Select options, and choose **Go To**.

2 Type the cell reference in the Reference box, as shown in Figure 2.2.

3 Press Enter and you go to that cell.

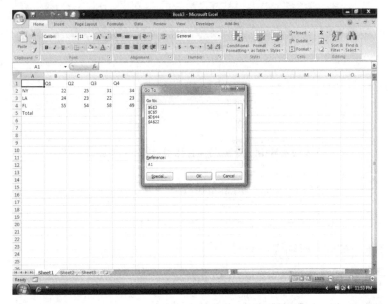

Figure 2.2
Using the Go To dialogue to jump around your spreadsheet.

Timesaver tip

One of the benefits of using the Go To dialogue over the Name Range is that your four most recent cell addresses are remembered in the Go To dialogue, so you can quickly return to any of those locations.

→ Worksheet Navigation Tricks

You can navigate quite easily using the mouse, the Name Box and/or the Go To button. You can also use the Find & Select options located on the Home tab. But here are a few tricks to help you get around a little faster:

■ Place your cursor anywhere in the worksheet. Then press Ctrl+Home and you will be brought right back to A1, the beginning of your worksheet.

■ To go to the beginning of the row you are currently in, select the Home key.

■ To repeat the previous action, press the F4 key. So, if you copy data and paste it into a cell and then want to repeat the pasting of that data, just select another cell and press F4. It will repeat the last action until you change that last action to something else.

■ To move to the bottom right-hand corner of a worksheet's data, press Ctrl+End.

■ If you have multiple worksheets in your workbook that you want to navigate through quickly, you can press Ctrl+Page Up or Page Down, depending on whether you want to scroll left or right through the sheets.

Go To Special

As mentioned above, the Go To dialogue allows you to quickly go to a cell address you provide. However, you can also use Go To Special (shown in Figure 2.3) to perform advanced navigation through your data.

You can see there is a list of different characteristics you can search for and when you select one, Excel will automatically select all the cells in your worksheet that match the list.

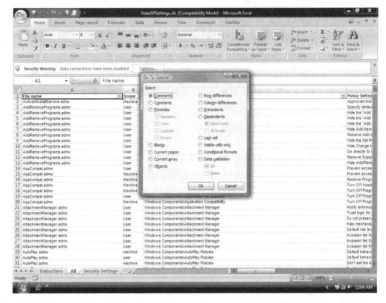

Figure 2.3
Using the Go To Special dialogue.

To use the Go To Special option, you perform the following:

1 Go to the Home ribbon, to the Editing Grouping, select the Find & Select option and choose **Go To Special**. Note: You could also open Go To and then choose the **Special** button.

2 Choose a specific type of special entry you are looking for. Each option has different results and can be used for a variety of reasons.

3 Once your items are highlighted you can jump from one point to the next by using your tab button.

Timesaver tip

Before using Go To Special, if you want to narrow down your search radius you can select the cell range that you want to have examined. If you don't choose one then Go To Special will examine the entire worksheet.

2

Important

You can choose Comments to find all the comments in your spreadsheet. Click Objects to locate charts, clip art, SmartArt and so forth. If you use Constants this will call upon all cells that don't have formulas (including text or numbers that are input as text). You can also search for formulas in your worksheet (and the type of formulas, including searching only for errors.) As you can see, the Go To Special options can take you to another level of Excel use.

→ Insert Different Types of Data

As mentioned earlier you can insert text, numbers, dates and so forth into a cell. Let's consider the steps for each of these.

Insert Text

Although a spreadsheet is all about the numbers and formulas, you need text to give meaning to those numbers. You use text to define column and row headings, or to explain certain results. Some Excel spreadsheets are not made up of numbers at all, but simply allow a way to display large tables of text, as shown in Figure 2.4.

Text entered will automatically be left-aligned (although numerical data is right-aligned). Text can be letters, characters, numbers and spaces.

Important

At times you may want to enter numbers that should be treated as text, for example a zip code like 08817. In these cases you can indicate this to Excel by using a single quotation mark (') before your entry. So, you would enter '08817 in your cell to ensure it being treated as text.

Figure 2.4
A large table that's made up primarily of textual information.

At times your text may not fit in the cell you are using. This will be handled in one of two ways. If the cell next to the one you are typing in is empty, the text will overflow into the others. If the cell is not empty, your text will be truncated and you would be able to see it only if you selected the cell and looked in the formula bar, as shown in Figure 2.5. You can fix this problem by changing the column width.

Working with Comments

At times you may wish to add comments into your Excel spreadsheet but you do not want these comments to actually take up cell space. These comments act like a Post-it note in allowing you to explain the contents of a particular cell or provide a reminder for the person reading the spreadsheet.

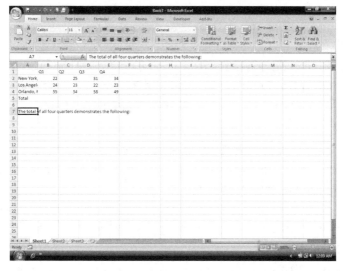

Figure 2.5
How text is handled when it is too long for the cell space.

Comments appear as little red triangles in the upper right corner of a cell (as shown in Figure 2.6) and you can view the content by placing your cursor over them.

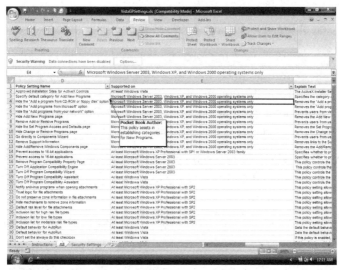

Figure 2.6
Adding comments to your worksheet.

To insert a comment into your spreadsheet, perform the following:

1 Select the cell you wish to add the comment to.

2 You can do one of the following: a) right-click and choose **Insert Comment**, or b) select the Review tab, under the Comments grouping, select **New Comment**, or c) hit Shift+F2.

3 You will notice the Excel user name is included in the comment. You type the text you want to add and then select anywhere else in the spreadsheet.

Important

To change the name of the Excel user shown in comments you need to select the Office Button, then Excel Options. This will bring you, by default, to the Popular settings and under the heading **Personalize your copy of Microsoft Office** you can change the **User name**.

To edit a comment, you perform the following:

1 Select the cell you wish to edit the comment from.

2 You can do one of the following: a) right-click and choose **Edit Comment** and then place your cursor in the comment box and edit the comment, or b) select the Review tab, under the Comments grouping, and select **Edit Comment** and then place your cursor in the comment box and edit the comment.

If your comments are set to be visible by default you can just click inside a comment box to edit the comment. To set a comment as visible, you perform the following:

1 Select the cell you wish to make the comment visible from.

2 You can do one of the following: a) right-click and choose **Show/Hide Comment**, or b) select the Review tab, under the Comments grouping, and select **Show/Hide Comment**.

3 If you wanted to see all comments (or hide all comments) on a worksheet at one time you can go to the Review tab, under the Comments grouping, and select or de-select "Show all comments".

To remove a comment, you perform the following:

1 Select the cell you wish to delete the comment from.

2 You can do one of the following: a) right-click and choose **Delete Comment**, or b) select the Review tab, under the Comments grouping, and select **Delete Comment**.

Insert Numerical Data

Data that serves as values in your Excel spreadsheet includes the numerical entries 0–9, as well as characters related to numerical data such as a dollar sign ($), percent sign (%), commas (,) and so forth.

You can enter your numerical data exactly as you wish it to be displayed (for example, you can type in the number $1,000.00) or you can enter the data directly and format the cells later (for example, you can type in the number 1000 and format the cells as currency).

To insert numerical data within a cell, perform the following:

1 Select the cell you wish to add data to.

2 Type in the value (exactly as you wish to see it, or in a plain style you can format later). Note: To use negative numbers you just have to put a minus sign (–) before the number.

3 Hit Enter or Tab and you will notice that the data is right-aligned, as shown in the chart in Figure 2.7.

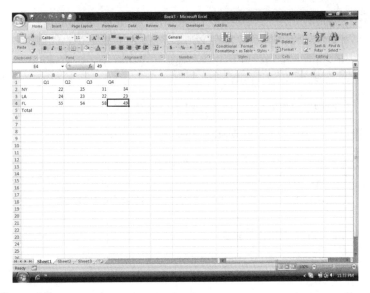

Figure 2.7
Entering numerical data in your worksheet.

Timesaver tip

Sometimes your numbers are too large to fit within their cells. In this case the number changes into a grouping of ###### signs (see Figure 2.8). You can manually make the column larger or you can double-click the right-hand border of the columns heading. The column will automatically expand to accommodate the largest number in that column.

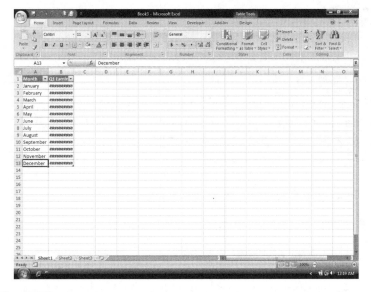

Figure 2.8
Handling the #### dilemma.

Insert Dates and Times

Dates and times inserted into Excel are viewed as values. For a date entry, the value is a number of days elapsed since January 1, 1900. For a time entry, the value is the number of seconds elapsed since 12 a.m. These values are not shown to you but Excel uses these hidden values when you use a date or time setting in a calculation.

To insert a date, you perform the following:

1 Select the cell you wish to add the date to.

2 Type the date using either slash marks MM/DD/YYYY (for example, 04/05/2007) or hyphens MM-DD-YY (for example 04-05-07), or DD-<name of month>-YYYY (for example, 05-April-2007).

3 Then hit Enter or Tab.

Timesaver tip

To insert the current date in a cell, type Ctrl+; (semicolon). To ensure the spreadsheet always uses the current date you can use the TODAY and/or NOW functions. (Functions will be discussed in Chapter 8.)

To insert the time, perform the following:

1 Select the cell you wish to add the time to.

2 For the time remember to include a.m. or p.m., otherwise Excel will think the time is a.m. automatically. To do this, type 6:00 a (for a.m.) and/or 6:00 p (for p.m.). If you want to use military time (aka the 24-hour international clock) you can type 6:00 (without the a) for 6 a.m. and 18:00 (without the p) for 6 in the evening.

3 Then hit Enter or Tab.

Timesaver tip

To insert the current time in a cell, type Ctrl+Shift+; (semicolon).

3

Automatic Data Entry Methods

In this lesson you will master the art of data entry by learning quicker, more automatic ways of filling in cells through a variety of methods, including cutting the data from one location and pasting into another, or using the AutoFill feature to populate your cells with data. You will also learn an important aspect to Exchange, how to select and work with ranges of data!

→ Selecting Ranges

You can work faster and more productively if you work with ranges of data, as opposed to working in one cell at a time.

Jargon buster

A **range** is the selection of two or more cells at a time.

Cell ranges can be contiguous or random. Contiguous cell ranges are selected in a rectangular region in one area where the cells are next to one another. You can also select individual cells, or groupings of cells to form a random range.

Excel uses cell addresses to identify the range. In the case of a contiguous range, it will use the top left cell for the first address and the bottom right cell for the end address, separated by a colon. In Figure 3.1 you see the contiguous range of B3:H9.

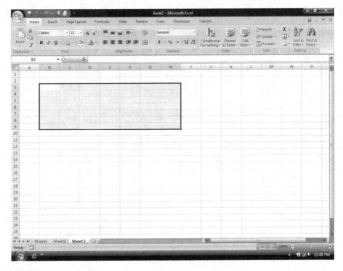

Figure 3.1
A contiguous range with the address B3:H9.

For a random range, commas are used to separate each portion. An example of a random range address would be B2,C8,D9:F13. This indicates two cells (B2 and C8) as part of the range and then a contiguous grouping of cells (D9:F13) as also being part of the range.

Important

Ranges can be used for many different reasons. You might select a range to copy a portion of your worksheet data. Or, in creating a formula, you might use a range of data (contiguous or non-contiguous) to complete the formula. You would also select a range of data to create a chart.

Select a Contiguous Range

To select a contiguous range of cells you perform the following:

1 Using your mouse, select the cell you wish to begin your range selection in.

2 Drag your mouse to the cell you wish to end your range selection in.

Note: The actual direction you drag your mouse pointer doesn't really matter. Usually you select a range from top left to bottom right, but you could select cell ranges in any direction you choose.

Select a Random Range

To select random ranges of cells, you perform the following:

1 Using your mouse, select the cell you wish to begin your range selection in.

2 Hold down the Ctrl key and select additional cells, groupings of cells and/or entire rows or columns until you have your range selected.

Timesaver tip

If you want to select an entire column, you just select the column heading(s). For rows, you can select the row(s). However, if you would like to select the entire worksheet, place your cursor in the little square box that separates the column and row headings. This is the **Select All** option for your worksheet.

Name a Range

Naming a range will make it easier for you to work with and remember later on in working with formulas in your spreadsheet. Instead of remembering B3:E6, you only have to remember **QuarterlyData**.

To name a range, perform the following:

1 Using your mouse, select the cell you wish to begin your range selection in.

2 Drag your mouse to the cell you wish to end your range selection in. (Or, if you are selecting a random range, hold Ctrl and complete your range selection.)

3 Once you have your range selected you can do one of the following: a) right-click within your range selection and choose the **Name a Range** option from your mini-toolbar, or b) go to the Formulas ribbon, to the Defined Names grouping and select the **Define Name** option.

4 In the **New Name** dialogue box (shown in Figure 3.2) you provide a name that relates to your selection, determine whether it applies to the entire workbook or just a specific worksheet, add comments as needed and select **OK**.

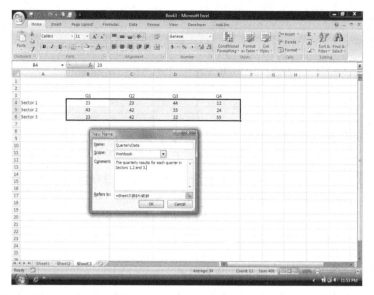

Figure 3.2
Naming your range.

Timesaver tip

You can quickly navigate to your named range by selecting the down
arrow of the Name Box and choosing your range name.

→ Insert Data into Multiple Cells Quickly

You don't always have to select a cell and enter the data directly.
There are many ways to increase your productivity with Excel by
filling in cells quickly with text, numbers and even formulas.

Use the Clipboard to Enter Data

One way to copy data from one cell or multiple cells to another
location is to use the Clipboard. To do this, perform the following:

1 Select the cell(s) you wish to copy.

2 Then from the Home ribbon, from the Clipboard grouping, select the Copy button. (Note: You could also select the cell(s) and hit Ctrl+C to copy or right-click and choose Copy from the mini-toolbar.)

3 Select the location within your worksheet (or in a separate worksheet or workbook) where you wish to paste your data.

4 Then, from the Home ribbon, from the Clipboard grouping, select the Paste button. (Note: You could also select hit Ctrl+V to paste, or right-click and choose Paste from the mini-toolbar.)

Use Ctrl+Enter to Enter Data

Often, though, you may want to enter the same data into multiple cells. For example, if you have cells that you need to return to and enter data in later on, you may want to put a 0 in those cells for now (or reminder text). To do this, you can perform the following:

1 Using your mouse, select the cell range (contiguous or non-contiguous) using the methods described earlier in this chapter.

2 Enter the text, number or formula you want repeated in the Formula Bar.

3 Hold Ctrl and hit Enter and you will see the information is entered into multiple cells.

Important

If you use Ctrl+Enter to add a formula to multiple cells, Excel will use relative cell references. If you want to use absolute values, before pressing Ctrl+Enter, select the cell reference and then hit F4.

Jargon buster

Absolute and relative cell references are used in formulas to determine whether the formula is locked into the cells that it has been provided or if, upon being moved, the cell range also moves. If the formula included a relative cell reference (for example, A1), then if you move the formula over, it will change its reference too. If you use an absolute cell reference (which is done with dollar signs, for example, A1), then you can move the formula and it will remain the same. Note: You can also create formulas that mix the reference, for example, $A1 is an absolute column, relative row reference. See Figure 3.3 for an example of each.

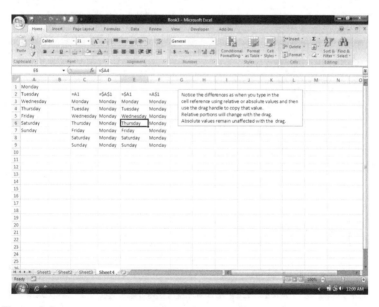

Figure 3.3
Absolute and relative cell references.

Use AutoFill to Enter Data

Sometimes you have data that needs to simply be repeated straight down a column or across a row. You can do this quickly using AutoFill. To do this, perform the following:

1 Insert data into a cell.

2 Click the fill handle of the cell, which is the small block in the lower right-hand corner, as shown in Figure 3.4.

3 Drag the handle down or to the right to make a copy of the data. You'll notice a data tag to show you exactly what is being copied.

4 Release the mouse button and the data is filled into those cells.

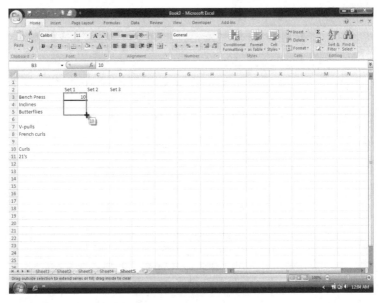

Figure 3.4
Using AutoFill to copy a single cell worth of data.

Use AutoFill to Enter a Series of Data

You can use the AutoFill feature to enter a value series of data (for example, Monday, Tuesday and so on). There are various ways to accomplish this. One way is to fill in a couple of cells to give Excel a reference point. You can perform the following:

1 Type Monday in cell A1.

2 Type Tuesday in cell A2.

3 Select cells A1 and A2 and then grab the data handle.

4 As you drag the data handle you will see that it will automatically continue the series (as shown in Figure 3.5).

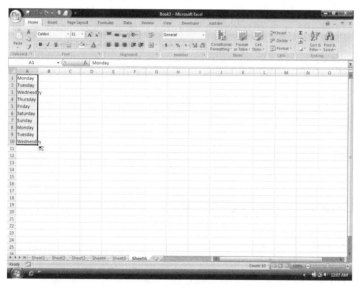

Figure 3.5
Using AutoFill to continue a series.

You can perform the same thing (only with a bit more functionality) using the AutoFill Options. To do this, perform the following:

1 Type Monday in cell A1.

2 Select cell A1 using the data handle and drag it down about 7 cells.

3 After releasing the mouse button you will see the AutoFill Options button. If you select that button you see the options in Figure 3.6.

4 Notice you can tell Excel to just copy the data (in which case Monday will be in all of those cells) or even Fill Weekdays (which will eliminate Saturday and Sunday from the series). As you can see, AutoFill attempts to be intuitive when creating your data series.

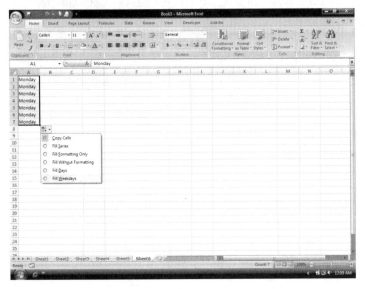

Figure 3.6
Using the AutoFill Options.

Excel can do this with any number of series, from straight numeric patterns to sequences such as the following:

■ Monday – Tuesday, Wednesday, Thursday, Friday, and so on.

■ Jan – Feb, Mar, Apr, and so on.

■ January – February, March, and so on.

■ Q1 – Q2, Q3, Q4, and so on.

- Qtr 1 – Qtr 2, Qtr 3, Qtr 4, Qtr 1, and so on.

- 1st period – 2nd period, 3rd period, 4th period, and so on.

- Oct 23 2006 – Oct 24 2006, Oct 25 2006, and so on.

Important

There is a trick to alter the way AutoFill works. Depending on the programmed pattern that AutoFill has set, if you hold the Ctrl button as you drag it will augment the default behaviour.

Creating Custom Series

If you type a 1 and drag the number with standard AutoFill you will get a string of 1s down the column. You can alter this by holding the Ctrl key and then the numbers increment by 1 down the column (i.e. 1, 2, 3 and so forth). However, if you would like to increment by numbers other than 1 at a time, you need to do the following:

1 Start by entering the first number in your series in a cell.

2 In the next cell, enter the next number in your increment so that Excel understands that you want to create a series of numbers to increment. For example, if you start with 100, then 200.

3 Then use the AutoFill feature by selecting both cells and dragging the fill handle until the series is complete.

Timesaver tip

You can create series of items other than numbers. For example, if you wanted every other month you would type January, March and then drag the fill handle. If you wanted every other day you would start with Sunday, Tuesday and drag the fill handle.

In addition to using the AutoFill feature to create a series, you can use the Series dialogue box, shown in Figure 3.7, to have greater control over your series increments.

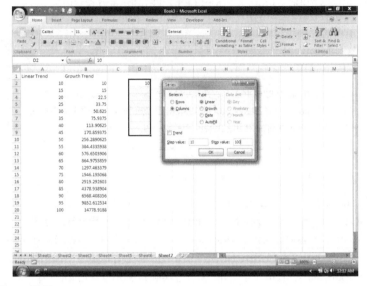

Figure 3.7
The Series dialogue box allows you to establish defined increments.

To use the Series dialogue box, you perform the following:

1 Select a cell and insert your starting point for series incrementation.

2 Go to the **Home** ribbon, to the **Editing** grouping and select the **Fill** button, and then choose **Series**.

3 You are presented with many options, but for a standard incrementation of data series from 10–100, by increments of 10 you would select **Column**, leave the default Linear setting and then type 10 in the Step Value and 100 in the Stop value.

4 Then hit OK and your cells should be incremented in series of 10.

Jargon buster

Linear trends will continue the series of data by adding the step value of your initial data cell. **Growth trends** will continue the series of data determining the percentage of difference between items in the series and then applying that difference to successive cells. This can be helpful in trying to project future growth patterns based upon your current growth percentages.

Timesaver tip

If you want quicker access to your Fill settings, hold down your right mouse button (instead of your left) when you drag your fill options. After letting go you will be presented with the Fill menu options, as shown in Figure 3.8.

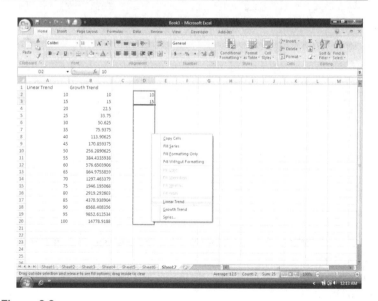

Figure 3.8
A quick way to see your Fill settings, including a quick way to have a linear or growth trend series.

→ AutoComplete

AutoComplete has been a useful tool in the Office suite for some time. It is especially useful in spreadsheet creation because Excel will keep track of all the labels you are using in a column. So, let's say you are entering the name of football teams from Brazil. You start with Sao Paulo, then Palmeiras, Corinthians and so forth. The next time you enter a P in a cell in that column, Excel will automatically enter "Palmeiras".

Another feature of AutoComplete is the ability to pick from a list of names in a column. You type in your list in a column and then at the bottom, right-click an empty cell and choose **Pick from Drop-Down List** (shown in Figure 3.9). Then choose your next label.

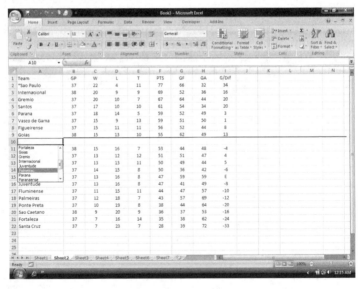

Figure 3.9
AutoComplete lets you quickly add labels and also presents a drop-down list.

4

Formatting Cells

In this lesson you will learn how to make that spreadsheet of yours pop off the screen. Spreadsheets don't have to be boring. You will learn how to change the font options of your text, manipulate the alignment of text, change the row/column height and width, and more to make your data easier to read.

→ Formatting Using the Font Grouping

Much like any data you plan on sharing with others, you need to use formatting techniques to make certain portions stand out. You can do this by bolding or underlining certain text. You can change the colour or the size of the font you are using, or even the font itself of the cell.

Jargon buster

A **font** is defined as a design for a set of characters. It is a combination of a typeface (such as Times New Roman) and other qualities (such as size, pitch and spacing). While the typeface defines the shape of the characters, you have many other things you can personally configure, such as the size, whether it is bold or italic and so forth.

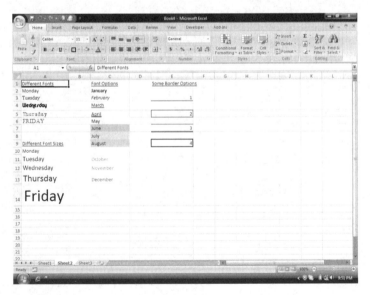

Figure 4.1
Basic font formatting.

As an example, Figure 4.1 shows several columns of text that display the features found under the Font grouping of the Home tab.

To change the basic font formatting, perform the following:

1 Select a cell or cell range that you wish to change the formatting for.

2 Select the Home ribbon and look at the Font grouping.

3 Choose one of the following:

- The **Font down** arrow to change the font type. There are many built-in fonts to choose from, including some new ones like Calibri or Cambria.

- The **Font Size** down arrow to make the font size smaller or larger.

- The **Grow Font** or **Shrink Font** buttons to quickly increase or decrease the size of your fonts.

- The **Bold**, **Italics** or **Underline** button. Note: You could select the down arrow next to the Underline button to see the Double Underline option.

- The **More Borders** selection, which gives you an impressive list of ways to add borders to your cells either automatically or through drawing tools.

- The **Fill Color** option, which shows you colours you can add to the cell background.

- The **Font Color** option, which lets you pick a different colour for your text.

Timesaver tip

If you like the way you have formatted a certain cell or grouping of cells, you can repeat the entire process over and over again. But an easier option would be for you to select a cell whose formatting you like, then go to the Home ribbon, the Clipboard grouping and select the Format Painter button. Select the new cell or cell grouping you wish to apply (or paint) that formatting towards.

→ Formatting Using the Format Cells Dialogue Box

If you would like to have a little more control over some of your formatting and prefer to work with the format cells dialogue (shown in Figure 4.2), you can perform the following:

1 Select a cell or cell range that you wish to change the formatting for.

2 Select the Home ribbon and look at the Font grouping. In the bottom right corner of the grouping is the dialogue launcher arrow. Select this option.

3 There are six tabs but only three correspond to the Font grouping. They are **Font**, **Border** and **Fill.** The buttons on the Home ribbon do not give you the maximum set of options that you find within these tabs.

Timesaver tip

For a quick way to open the Format Cells dialogue box, just hit Ctrl+1.

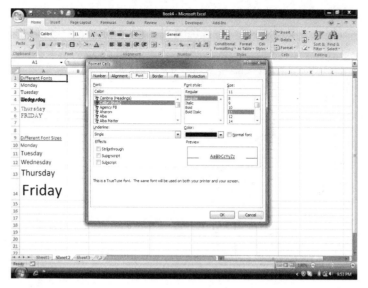

Figure 4.2
Font formatting with the Format Cells dialogue.

Timesaver tip

The mini-toolbar is another way to perform quick formatting of your cell or cell grouping. You select the cell or cell grouping and right-click. The mini-toolbar (shown in Figure 4.3) shows you a grouping of cell formatting options. Beneath the toolbar is a menu of other actions you can perform quickly.

→ Formatting Using the Alignment Grouping

There is a variety of ways you may want to align your data within a cell. Sometimes you may want it centred, other times you may even want to put it sideways or on an angle. Figure 4.4 shows different alignment options you may wish to try with your cell data.

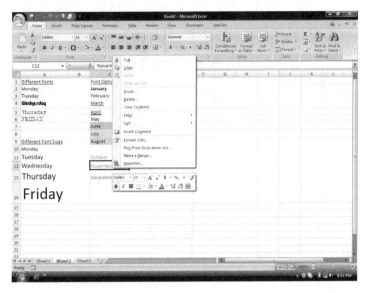

Figure 4.3
Working with the mini-toolbar.

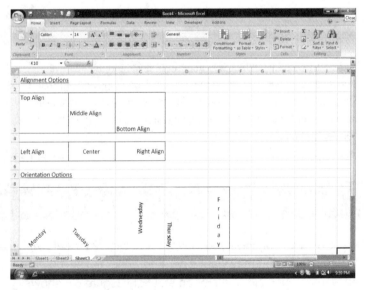

Figure 4.4
Cell alignment possibilities.

To work with the Alignment grouping, perform the following:

1 Select a cell or cell range that you wish to change the formatting for.

2 Select the Home ribbon and look at the Alignment grouping.

3 Choose one of the following:

- The Top, Middle or Bottom Align buttons to determine where in your cell the text will be positioned vertically.

- The Align text Left, Center or Right buttons to determine where in your cell the text will be positioned horizontally.

- The Orientation options to provide you with standard text rotation so that you can place your text at angles.

- The Decrease or Increase Indent options to alter the indenting options.

- The Wrap Text button to allow your text to wrap within the cell instead of being cut off or pushing into other cells.

- The Merge Center to let you configure merging of cells.

Important

If you create a table in Word you will notice that your only options for text alignment are horizontal or vertical (no rotation of text options). To have a table in Word with rotated headings you can create it in Excel and then copy it and Paste Special into Word using Microsoft Excel Worksheet Object as your option.

→ Alignment Options from the Format Cells Dialogue

While the Home ribbon, Alignment grouping gives you plenty of options to work from, you may want to perform more intricate alignment operations. For example, you may want to configure a more detailed angle for your text, beyond that provided from the Home ribbons options.

To carry out more detailed alignment operations, perform the following:

1 Select a cell or cell range that you wish to change the cell alignment for.

2 Select the Home ribbon and look at the Alignment grouping. In the bottom right corner of the grouping is the dialogue launcher arrow. Select this option.

3 From the Format Cells dialogue, on the Alignment tab (shown in Figure 4.5) you can configure the same options as from the ribbon with some added control (i.e. you can set the degree of alignment).

Important

A check box on the Alignment tab called "Shrink to fit" has a great effect on your formatting. This option will allow Excel to automatically adjust the font size of the cell if the contents are too wide. It will not change formatting but scaling, incrementing 1 point at a time. Use this option sparingly, however, because you do not want your spreadsheet to look too awkward with different sizes in each cell.

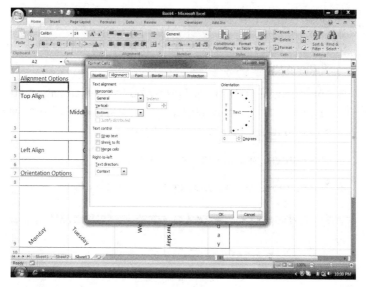

Figure 4.5
Cell alignment configuraton settings.

→ Formatting Using the Number Grouping

You can alter the appearance of a number without changing the number itself. You do this using different number formats.

A quick and easy way to change the number format is through the Home ribbon, Number grouping. You are provided with a mini-gallery of options that allows you to configure dates, currency, fractions and so forth.

To quickly alter the number format, perform the following:

1 Select a cell or cell range that you wish to change the formatting for.

2 Select the Home ribbon and look at the Number grouping.

3 Choose one of the following:

■ The Number Format down arrow, which provides a listing of quick options (shown in Figure 4.6).

■ The Accounting Number Format button, which allows you to choose the form of currency (dollars, pounds, euros and so forth) to append to the number.

■ The percent or comma style buttons.

■ The increase or decrease decimal point buttons.

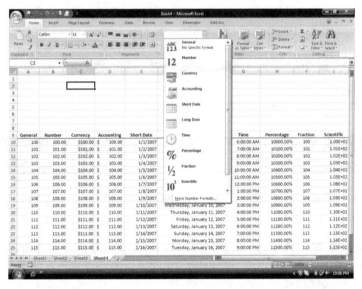

Figure 4.6
The Number Format options from the Home ribbon.

→ Number Options from the Format Cells Dialogue

While the Home ribbon, Number grouping gives you some formatting options, a more elaborate set of options can be found from the Format Cells dialogue box, under the Number tab (shown in Figure 4.7).

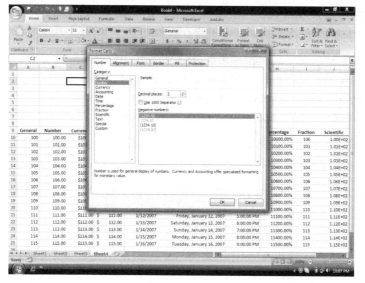

Figure 4.7
The Number Format options from the Format Cells dialogue box.

Here is a list of options for each setting:

■ *General*: This is the default setting and will usually format the numbers exactly as you type them. It will automatically use scientific notation for numbers that go beyond 12 digits.

■ *Number*: For generic number displays including settings for decimal places, using a comma as a thousand separator and choices on negative number display.

■ *Currency*: Similar in nature to the Number format but with the added configuration options that relate to monetary symbol formatting. Note: If you input a number and use a dollar sign, Excel will automatically apply the Currency format.

■ *Accounting*: Similar to the Currency format but aligns the currency symbols or decimal points in columns.

■ *Date*: Allows you to configure how you want your date displayed (for example, 7/5/2007 or July 5th, 2007 and so forth).

- *Time*: Allows you to configure how you want your time displayed (for example, 9:30 or 21:30).

- *Percentage*: Multiplies the cell value by 100 and uses a percent symbol. You can configure the number of decimal places. If you input a number and use a percent sign, Excel will automatically apply the Percentage format.

- *Fraction*: Displays the number as a fraction according to the type you specify (for example, as halves or quarters and so forth).

- *Scientific*: Uses exponential notation, replacing part of the number with E+n, where E multiplies the preceding number by 10 to the nth power.

- *Text*: Allows you to type anything, even numbers, and it will be formatted as text.

- *Special*: Allows you to choose options like postal code or social security number.

- *Custom*: Allows you to modify a copy of an existing number format.

Important

Date and time formats that begin with an asterisk (*) respond to changes in regional date and time settings that are specified in Windows Control Panel (in Windows Vista these are under Regional and Language Options). Formats without an asterisk are not affected by Control Panel settings.

→ Format Row Height and Column Width

On a new worksheet, every row is exactly 12.75 points high and every column is 8.43 characters wide. But there are times when you need to adjust these settings to make your spreadsheet easier to manage. At times these adjustments come automatically (like when you change the font size of a cell and the row size adjusts accordingly). Other times you may want to manually adjust these settings.

You can use one of the following to adjust row height or column widths:

■ *Excel AutoFit*: By double-clicking the right border of a column or the bottom border of a row, Excel will automatically expand (or shrink) the column or row to the widest or tallest entry. Selecting multiple rows or columns allows you to do this all at once.

■ *Click and Drag*: You can select the column or row and then use your mouse to select the lines on the column or row heading once your mouse cursor becomes a two-headed arrow. You can drag the size until you are happy with it and then release the mouse button. Note: While dragging your mouse you will be shown a screen tip that gives you the size of your row or column in both characters (for columns) and points (for rows) as well as in pixels.

■ *For greater precision you can also select a column or row.* Then from the Home ribbon, the Cells grouping you can choose the Format down arrow. Choose Row Height or Column Width to provide exact sizes – for columns, a number between 0 and 255 (for characters), for rows, a number between 0 and 409 (in points). Note: You can also see this dialogue if you right-click a column or row and choose "Row Height" or "Column Width".

Hide/Unhide Rows and Columns

You may have data in your spreadsheet that you wish to hide from the view of others, or even from yourself so you can analyse data differently. To do this, perform the following:

1 Select an entire row or an entire column by selecting its heading label.

2 From the Home ribbon, under the Cells grouping select the down arrow for the Format button. Under your Visibility section you have the Hide & Unhide settings that allow you to hide/unhide a row, a column, or an entire worksheet.

3 Select the one you want and it will look as if it has disappeared.

Note: You could also have the column width or row height set to 0 to make it disappear. Or you can right-click a column or row and choose the Hide/Unhide options.

5

Excel Styles and Themes

In this lesson you will learn how to use styles (both those included in Excel, and those you personally create) to quickly and easily improve the look of your Excel spreadsheets. In addition, you will learn about Themes, a new feature of Office 2007 that allows you to have a unified presentation look between your Word, Excel and PowerPoint documentation.

→ Using a Cell Style

There are times when you don't want to take the time to figure out a formatting scheme for your cells but do not want to forfeit the look of your worksheet. You can use a preconfigured cell **style** to quickly enhance the presentation of your data.

To see a gallery of options for cell styles (shown in Figure 5.1), you perform the following:

1 Select a cell or cell range that you wish to change the cell style for.

2 On the Home ribbon, under the Styles grouping, select the Cell Styles down arrow.

3 As you move your cursor over different style options, notice how the cells update their look in real time through a **live preview** by applying the gallery option you hover your mouse over.

4 Select an option to apply it to the cell or cell range.

You'll notice that the Cell Styles Gallery is organised into helpful groupings that you can use to format your worksheet appropriately. For example, there is a **Titles and Headings** section and a **Themed Cell Styles** section.

→ Create Your Own Cell Styles

While the Cell Styles Gallery allows you to apply a style quickly, it may not be "your" style or that of your company. Your company may have a specific look it wants applied to its spreadsheets. But the Styles Gallery is designed to be improved upon and added to.

You can create a new style or modify an existing one.

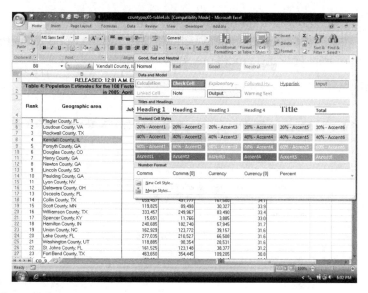

Figure 5.1
The Cell Styles Gallery.

Create a New Style

To create a new style, perform the following:

1 Select a cell and apply the formatting you want to use again in the future. Note, you can format the number, alignment, font, border, fill and protection aspects of the cell.

2 On the Home ribbon, under the Styles grouping, select the Cell Styles down arrow.

3 At the bottom of the gallery you can choose the **New Cell Style** option and you will be presented with a Style dialogue box, shown in Figure 5.2.

4 Provide a name for your style.

5 You can opt not to include certain aspects of the formatting by de-selecting any of the formatting categories.

6 If you choose the **Format** button you will be taken to the **Format Cells** dialogue, which will give you the opportunity to modify your style more precisely.

7 When you have your style just right, select the OK button.

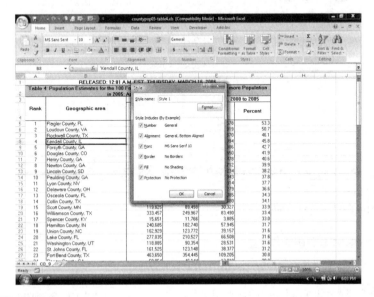

Figure 5.2
Creating a new cell style.

Once your new style is created, to apply it to cells in your worksheet you just have to select those cells and go to the Styles Gallery. You'll notice that there is now a Custom heading with your custom-made styles right at the top.

Modify an Existing Style

You can modify any of the styles in your gallery, both those that were preconfigured for you and those that you created personally.

To modify a pre-existing style, perform the following:

1 On the Home ribbon, under the Styles grouping, select the Cell Styles down arrow.

2 Right-click the cell style you wish to modify (preconfigured or custom). Note the options to Modify, Duplicate and Delete (as shown in Figure 5.3). Choose **Modify**.

3 You can change the name of your style.

4 You can de-select certain aspects of the formatting by de-selecting any of the formatting categories.

5 If you choose the **Format** button you will be taken to the **Format Cells** dialogue, which will give you the opportunity to modify your style more precisely.

6 When you have your style just right, select the OK button.

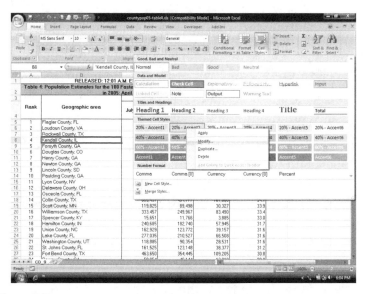

Figure 5.3
Style modification options.

Timesaver tip

If you want to create a new cell style that is similar to an existing one, you just have to right-click that style, select Duplicate, give it a new name and then modify the style to your specifications.

→ Using Table Styles

Individual cell styling gives you greater control over the look of your worksheet, but the next level of formatting relates to the look of an entire table. Excel 2007 offers you a Table Styles Gallery (shown in Figure 5.4) with the Live Preview feature so you can see what a table style will ultimately look like before applying it.

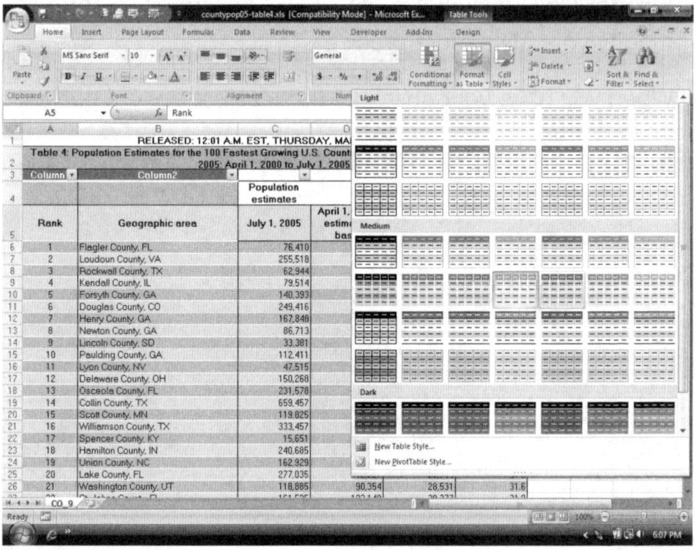

Figure 5.4
Table Styles Gallery.

Apply a Table Style from the Gallery

You can add a table style to a new table or one you have already created. In either case you select the columns and rows you want to format and then perform the following:

1 On the Home ribbon, under the Styles grouping, select the Format as Table down arrow.

2 Notice, there are Light, Medium and Dark styles to choose from (although there will be a Custom category if you have created your own). Hover your cursor above a style to see a live preview of how that style will look in your worksheet.

3 Select a style.

If you already have a table and want to change the formatting, you could place your cursor in the table and then select the Design contextual ribbon. On the Design ribbon under the Table Styles grouping (shown in Figure 5.5), you can select a style from the gallery to apply to that existing table.

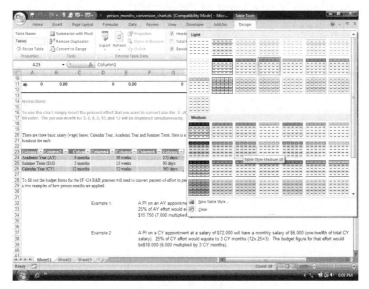

Figure 5.5
Table Styles Gallery from the Design ribbon.

Create Your Own Table Style

There are many ways to create your own style. You can take an existing style, duplicate it and then modify some of the aspects of the style. If you want to create a table style from scratch, you perform the following:

1 On the Home ribbon, under the Styles grouping, select the Format as Table down arrow.

2 Select the **New Table Style** option.

3 The New Table Quick Style dialogue will appear, as shown in Figure 5.6.

4 Give your style a name in the Name box.

5 From your Table Element options you can select any element and then click Format.

6 There will be three tabs (Font, Border and Fill) that you can use to format the options you like. Notice that your choices will then update Preview of your custom table style.

7 Once you have altered all the elements you want to, you can choose OK and your new style will appear under the Custom heading.

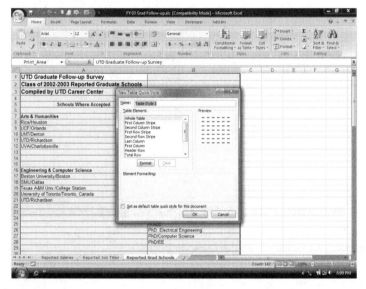

Figure 5.6
Creating a custom table style.

Apply, Modify, Duplicate and Delete a Table Style

There are different ways to apply a table style so that you have greater control over your worksheet. To see some of your options in working with a particular style you place your cursor over that style and right-click, as shown in Figure 5.7. Note: If you right-click a pre-existing table style, as opposed to a custom-made style, the Modify and Delete options will be grayed out.

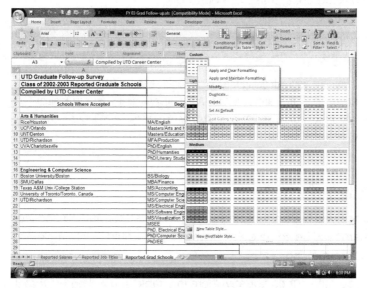

Figure 5.7
Working with table styles.

Notice in applying a style you can choose one of the following:

■ *Apply and Clear Formatting*: This will eliminate any prior cell formatting you have done, whether it is a simple bold format to certain cells, or even cell styles that you have applied.

■ *Apply (and Maintain Formatting)*: If you select this option, all your cell formatting for the table will remain intact, only the primary style of the table will change.

In creating new table styles the other right-click options can be most helpful. You can modify a custom-made style. You can duplicate a pre-existing style and then modify it to your liking. Or you can delete a custom-made style.

If you decide to select the **Set As Default** option for any of the table styles, that style will automatically be applied whenever you insert a table by choosing the Insert ribbon and selecting the Tables grouping, the Table button.

Timesaver tip

If you find yourself using the Cell or Table styles options often, you can right-click a style and select the Add Gallery to Quick Access Toolbar option. This will offer you a quick way to display the gallery, regardless of which ribbon you are working in.

Table Style Options

Once you have a table created with styled formatting applied, there may be some quick changes you would like to make to that formatting.

If you put your cursor anywhere in a table you will notice that the contextual ribbon Design appears in your ribbon tabs. Select the Design ribbon and look for the Table Style Options grouping, shown in Figure 5.8.

You can quickly select/de-select any of these options with one click to turn certain formatting options on or off. These are your options and their effect:

■ *Header Row*: If a table has a header row, this will turn it on and off.

■ *Total Row*: Can quickly add a total row to a table. The *subtotal* formula will automatically be added in for you.

■ *Banded Rows*: Turns the formatting borders across the rows on or off.

■ *First Column*: Will give the first column of the table special formatting to make it stand out.

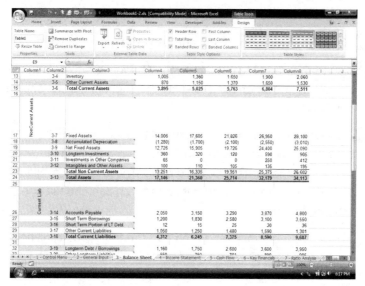

Figure 5.8
Table Style Options settings.

- *Last Column*: Will give the last column of the table special formatting to make it stand out.

- *Banded Columns*: Turns the formatting borders down the columns on or off.

→ Using Themes

On the Page Layout ribbon there is a grouping called Themes which is a new feature for the 2007 Office suite. The same grouping can be found in Word and PowerPoint (and, in general, these applications have a greater use for this feature). The purpose of the Themes grouping is to allow you to establish a look or style for your document that can be quickly applied in another application as well. This will create a professional, unified look to your presentations.

To apply a theme to your workbook, perform the following:

1 Open the workbook you want to apply a theme towards.

2 Go to the Page Layout tab, to the Themes grouping and select the down arrow to display the Themes gallery (shown in Figure 5.9).

3 Notice the many themes you have to choose from. In addition, you can create your own custom themes or download new ones from Microsoft. These will be available in Word, Excel and PowerPoint so that you can choose one theme for unity.

4 Hover your cursor over a theme to see the effect it will have over your worksheet. You will be able to see the results clearly if you have a worksheet that includes tables, charts and/or SmartArt. The colour and design layout will change with the live preview.

5 Select a theme you wish to use.

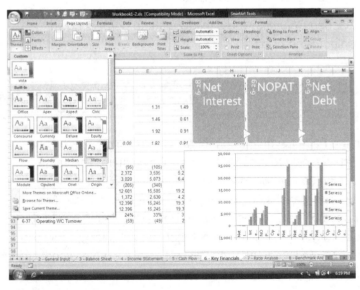

Figure 5.9
Choosing a theme for your Excel documents.

Important

You can modify a theme and then save it under a different theme name by altering the colours, fonts and theme effects from the Themes grouping on the Page Layout ribbon. Remember that themes are available in all three Office applications (Word, Excel and PowerPoint) so that you can unify your presentation style.

5

6

Conditional Formatting

In this lesson you will learn how Excel can format parts of a worksheet based upon conditions that you supply. Using colour scales and icon sets, you can create a graphical representation of the data at a glance using Conditional Formatting.

→ What is Conditional Formatting?

There are times when you are looking at a table of data with questions about the data (positive and negative traits) and the answers just aren't apparent. Conditional formatting attempts to make certain aspects of your data more colourful by using data bars, colour scales, icon sets and so forth.

The concept is simple. Depending on the condition that you determine, if a condition is true, one set of formatting is applied; if the condition is false, another set of formatting is applied or no formatting at all.

One example of conditional formatting would be a highlight alarm format. Let's say you have a column of data that shows the sales totals for your employees. You want all employees to sell at least £50,000 per month. If an employee's total is less than that amount, you want the figure to be red; if it is higher than that amount, you want it to be green. This will help you to quickly see which employees are worthy of commendation and which may require further assistance to reach their goal.

The type of conditional formatting you choose will be determined by the visual results you are looking for. For example, test results below 70% turn red. You can even use an icon to represent certain results.

Important

There are many creative ways to use conditional formatting. The Excel development team has a blog site that contains a ton of great information on improving your use of this feature. It can be found at **http://blogs.msdn.com/excel**

→ Formatting a Data Bar

Although this may seem complicated at first, once you see how easy they've made it you will feel more comfortable. Let's begin with a simple data bar format.

Jargon buster

A **data bar** is a visualisation of the data that allows you to quickly see the value of one cell's data in relation to other cells in the selection.

Apply Conditional Formatting: A Data Bar

To create a data bar format, perform the following:

1 Select a cell or cell range that you wish to apply conditional formatting towards. For example, in Figure 6.1 we use a range of numbers from 10 to 100 in increments of 10.

2 On the Home ribbon, under the Styles grouping, select the Conditional Formatting option.

3 Move your mouse down to the Data Bars.

4 Choose a colour option and you will see how your data is now represented with a visual bar from lower to higher.

This type of conditional format makes it easy to see the large and small numbers in a range. It becomes even more useful when you are working with a larger data range.

Advanced Data Bar Configuration

There are default settings for your data bar formatting, but you can go beyond these settings to choose different colours and different minimum or maximum values for the range.

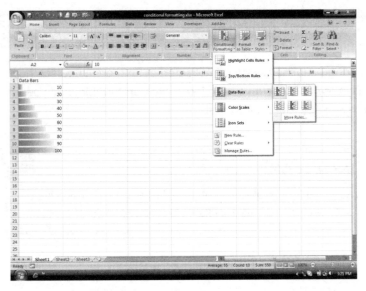

Figure 6.1
Data Bars.

To work with more advanced settings, perform the following:

1 Select a cell or cell range that you wish to apply conditional formatting towards.

2 On the Home ribbon, under the Styles grouping, select the Conditional Formatting option.

3 Move your mouse down to the Data Bars.

4 Select the **More Rules** option and you will be presented with the New Formatting Rule dialogue box, shown in Figure 6.2.

5 From here you can see the **Select a Rule Type**, but you do not want to make changes to these because you already have the data bar formatting option in mind.

6 Look down to the **Edit the Rule Description** portion of the dialogue. The current style is **Data Bar**, but you can alter this to use one of the other styles (like an icon set).

7 If you select the **Show Bar Only** checkbox, your data will not appear with the data bar in the cell. You will be able to edit the data, however, through the formula bar.

8 You can change the Shortest and Longest Bar values to work from a different set of rules.

9 Although the data bar gallery offers you only six choices, you can select a different colour to use for your data bars under the **Bar Colour** options.

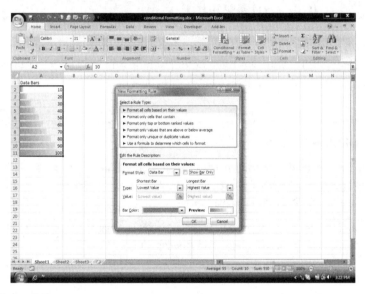

Figure 6.2
Advanced data bar options.

The best way to get the full value out of these different conditional formatting options is to test them out and see how they work one at a time. That will give you a better idea of how to apply them within your workbooks.

Important

You may be tempted to over-use conditional formatting in your workbook, but remember, it is a feature that is best used sparingly. It's meant to make certain features of your worksheet stand out with touches of colour.

→ Format with Colour Scales and Icon Sets

Data bars are just one of the new conditional formatting features in Excel 2007. You also have colour scales and icon sets to make your data easier to analyse.

Jargon buster

A **colour scale** is a gradient colour-shading format that changes the appearance of the scale based upon the data value of the cell in relation to other cells in the selection.

An **icon set** analyses the data in the selection and places an icon next to the data to indicate graphically your comparison.

Colour Scales

To create a colour scale conditional format, perform the following:

1 Select a cell or cell range that you wish to apply conditional formatting towards. For example, in Figure 6.3 we use a range of numbers from 10 to 100 in increments of 10.

2 On the Home ribbon, under the Styles grouping, select the Conditional Formatting option.

3 Move your mouse down to Color Scales.

4 Choose a colour option and you will see how your data is now represented by a colour that increments in intensity from lower to higher depending on the colour scheme you have chosen.

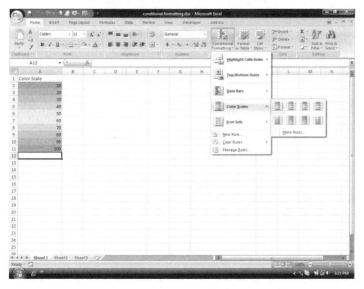

Figure 6.3
A colour scale.

As with the other conditional formats, you can create your own formatting rules for colour scales by selecting **More Rules** from the Conditional Formatting options under the Color Scales dropdown list.

Icon Sets

Icon sets allow you to choose from a variety of graphical icons (shown in Figure 6.4) to represent visually the value of a cell in relation to other selected cells.

To create an icon set conditional format, perform the following:

1 Select a cell or cell range that you wish to apply conditional formatting towards. For example, in Figure 6.5 we use a range of numbers from 10 to 100 in increments of 10.

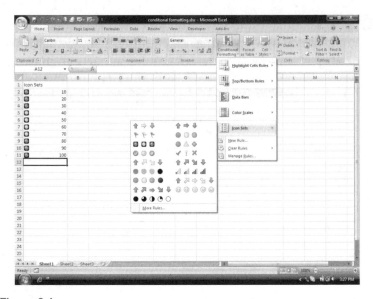

Figure 6.4
Icon set options.

2 On the Home ribbon, under the Styles grouping, select the Conditional Formatting option.

3 Move your mouse down to the Icon Sets.

4 Choose an icon pattern and you will see how your data is now represented by an icon that quickly demonstrates a positive, neutral or negative position in relation to the rest of your data.

As with the other conditional formats, you can create your own formatting rules for icon sets by selecting **More Rules** from the Conditional Formatting options under the Icon Sets dropdown list, shown in Figure 6.5.

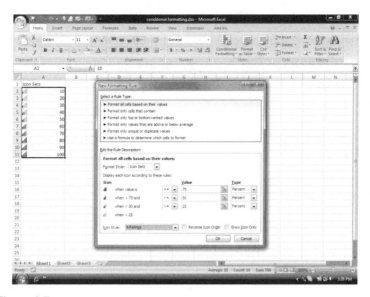

Figure 6.5
More Rules for icon sets.

Timesaver tip

Before choosing any of the conditional formatting options, remember that these all provide live preview so you can see how your colours or icons will look in your selected range.

→ Highlight Cells Rules

You can have greater control over your conditional formatting by creating conditions that you define and apply to your data selection that will create a reaction in your data if certain cells match the conditions.

Cells that meet the predefined conditions can be configured to change the colour of the font, or change to a different font style (bold, italics, underline, strikethrough, borders and so forth). The only things you cannot alter are the actual font type and size.

To use Highlight Cells Rules, perform the following:

1 Select a cell or cell range that you wish to apply conditional formatting towards. For example, in Figure 6.6 we use a range of complex numbers from a population survey.

2 On the Home ribbon, under the Styles grouping, select the Conditional Formatting option.

3 Move your mouse down to the Highlight Cells Rules options.

4 You can choose from a variety of comparison options. Each option will contain a corresponding dialogue box to help you define the conditions for your formatting. Your options include the following:

■ Greater Than

■ Less Than

■ Between

■ Equal To

■ Text That Contains

■ A Date Occurring

■ Duplicate Values

5 You can establish more than one rule for your data selection and can either accept the default colour options or create your own.

As with the other conditional formats, you can create your own formatting rules for icon sets by selecting **More Rules** from the Conditional Formatting options under the Highlight Cells Rules dropdown list.

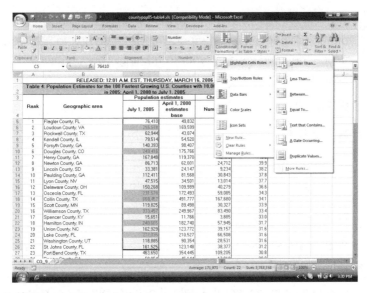

Figure 6.6
Working with Highlight Cells Rules.

→ Top/Bottom Rules

A quick way to see which figures are at the top or bottom of your selected range is to use the Top/Bottom conditional formatting rules.

To use Top/Bottom Rules, perform the following:

1 Select a cell or cell range that you wish to apply conditional formatting towards.

2 On the Home ribbon, under the Styles grouping, select the Conditional Formatting option.

3 Move your mouse down to the Top/Bottom Rules options.

4 You can choose from a variety of comparison options. Each option will contain a corresponding dialogue box to help you define the conditions for your formatting. Your options include the following:

- ■ Top 10 Items

- ■ Top 10%

- ■ Bottom 10 Items

- ■ Bottom 10%

- ■ Above Average

- ■ Below Average

5 You can establish more than one rule for your data selection and can either accept the default colour options or create your own.

As with the other conditional formats, you can create your own formatting rules for icon sets by selecting **More Rules** from the Conditional Formatting options under the Top/Bottom dropdown list.

→ Manage Multiple Conditional Formatting Rules

The application of more than one formatting rule can make modifications of those rules difficult. There are a few tools that make this easier.

To start with, if you want to remove all the rules in a selected area of your worksheet, or the entire worksheet, table or pivot table, you have an option to do this. Under the Conditional Formatting options you select the **Clear Rules** option and choose the extent of the removal.

If you have multiple rules applied to one selection, you can revise the conditions for those rules by looking under the Conditional Formatting options for the **Manage Rules** option shown in Figure 6.7.

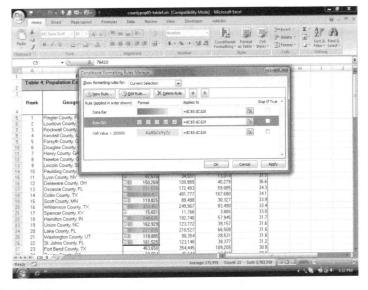

Figure 6.7
Manage Rules.

Important

If you apply multiple conditional formatting rules to a selection and notice that you aren't seeing the result you need, check your Manage Rules options to see the order of the rules you have defined. When multiple conditions apply to a cell, Excel will apply the format of the first true condition met and ignore the other rules. So, if one rule is more important to you than another, move that one up higher in the list by using the up and down arrows.

7

Basic Excel Formulas

In this lesson you will learn the basics of using formulas within your spreadsheets. Excel allows you to use a variety of standard operators (+, -, *, /) to create mini-formulas for everyday use.

→ What is a Formula?

Typing numbers into an Excel worksheet and formatting rows and columns might make Excel sound like a glorified table-making application. But Excel does much more by allowing you to insert formulas into your cells to perform both simple and complex calculations.

Jargon buster

A **formula** is an equation that begins with an equals (=) sign and can perform calculations within your worksheet based upon data you input directly into the formula, or based upon data that you reference from other portions of your worksheet. Basic formulas may include addition, subtraction, multiplication and/or division. More complex formulas might include financial and statistical functions (discussed further in Chapter 8).

Formulas are made up of some or all of the following:

■ *Functions*: A predetermined formula that takes the values you provide and performs the operation you choose (depending on the function) and returns a final value.

■ *References*: Rather than typing in numbers that already exist in another part of your worksheet, you can use a reference to the cell number.

■ *Constants*: Values that you specifically type into the formula.

■ *Operators*: Help you to add, subtract and so forth.

For example, consider the following formula:

=SUM(A1:A5)+A7/2

In this example we know it is a formula because we see the equals sign to start with. SUM is a function. A1:A5 provides the cell range that the SUM function would focus on. + and / are operators that add and divide. A7 is a reference and 2 is a constant.

→ Operators

There are many different types of calculation operators. Table 7.1 lists some primary arithmetic examples you need to know:

Table 7.1 Arithmetic Operators

Operator	Action	Example	Explanation
+	Addition	=A1+B1	Adds the values of A1 and B1 and returns a total
–	Subtraction	=A1–B1	Subtracts the value of B1 from A1
*	Multiplication	=A1*B1	Multiplies the values of A1 and B1
/	Division	=A1/B1	Divides the value of A1 by B1
^	Exponentiation	=A1^2	Raises the value of A1 to the 2nd power

In addition to standard arithmetic operators you can use comparison operators to compare values and produce either a True or False response. Table 7.2 lists some comparison operators you need to know:

Table 7.2 Comparison Operators

Operator	Action	Example	Explanation
=	Equal	A1=C1	The values of cells A1 and C1 are equal
>	Greater than	A1>C1	The value of A1 is greater than the value of C1
<	Less than	A1<C1	The value of A1 is less than the value of C1
>=	Greater than or equal to	A1>=C1	The value of A1 is greater than or equal to the value of C1
<=	Less than or equal to	A1<=C1	The value of A1 is less than or equal to the value of C1
<>	Not equal to	A1<>C1	The value of A1 is not equal to the value of C1

Combining Operators Properly

Much like standard mathematical calculations, there is an order that is applied to the formula. Excel reads the formula from left to right, but there is an order to each operator of the formula.

For example, consider the following formula:

=2+3*5

Ordinarily you might think to add 2 and 3 (equalling 5) and then multiply 5 by 5, producing 25. However, this would be incorrect. Because of the precedence rules among operators, the 3 would be multiplied by 5 (equalling 15) and then add 2 for a total of 17.

The natural order for operations is the following:

■ First, exponents (^) and parentheses.

■ Second, multiplication and division.

■ Third, addition and subtraction.

To clarify which portions of a formula you want addressed first you can use parentheses to alter the order. For example, consider the same formula as above but with the parentheses added:

=(2+3)*5

In the example above we get the result of 25. The parentheses make the addition complete first and then the multiplication.

Consider a more complicated example:

=(A1+B1)*(C1−D1)

In the example above, the operations in parentheses will complete first and then both values will be multiplied for a final value.

Important

You can nest parentheses within each other and Excel will evaluate these from the inside out. For example, =5*(3*(8+1)/2) would be addressed from the inner-most parentheses first. Meaning, 8 + 1 = 9, and then 3 * 9 = 27, divided by 2 = 13.5, and then finally multiplied by 5 = 67.5. With a formula you have no restriction on the number of parentheses you can use; however, with the use of a function you are limited to 64.

Timesaver tip

With larger formulas that hold many different parentheses it might become difficult to follow which portions are nested into other portions. Excel can assist in making this clearer for you. If you select within the formula itself, Excel will make parentheses take on different colours. As you move your cursor through the formula, your parentheses will become bolder to show you the opening and closing portions.

→ Enter and Edit Formulas

To enter a simple formula, perform the following:

1 Select a cell for the formula.

2 Type an equals sign (=) to start the formula.

3 Type the formula. For your first one try something simple like =2+2.

4 Hit Enter when you are done and you will see the results are located in your selected cell.

To enter a formula that includes cell addresses, perform the following:

1 Select a cell for the formula.

2 Type an equals sign (=) to start the formula.

3 Type the formula using the cell addresses, as shown in Figure 7.1. Note in the figure that this is a simple calculation but one that can be quite valuable when creating a spreadsheet to calculate a purchase price based upon quantity.

4 Hit Enter when you are done and you will see the results are located in your selected cell.

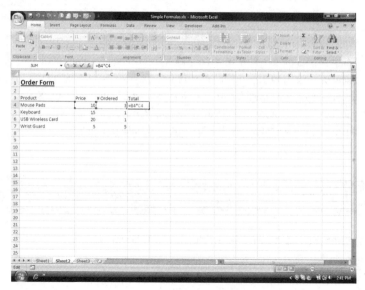

Figure 7.1
Entering a formula with cell addresses.

Important

Recall in Chapter 3 we discussed the use of absolute and relative values. This remains an important subject as you establish formulas. Relative cell addresses will change if you try to copy and move your reference. However, for items that you want to reference that need to stay constant, use an absolute cell address (one that uses $ to indicate a column and/or row address).

To enter a formula with cell addresses you select, perform the following:

1 Select a cell for the formula.

2 Type an equals sign (=) to start the formula.

3 Select a range of cells (as a way to practise this method). Then add an operator (+, −, *, /).

4 Select another range of cells.

5 Select Enter.

Notice that you can select ranges of cells quickly that become part of your formulas.

View Your Formula

You'll notice that your formula disappears when you finish entering it. To see the formula within a cell, you select the cell and the formula will appear in the formula bar (but you'll notice that the results will still be displayed in your cell, as shown in Figure 7.2).

If you select the cell holding a formula *twice*, your cursor will be in the cell and your formula will show in the cell directly.

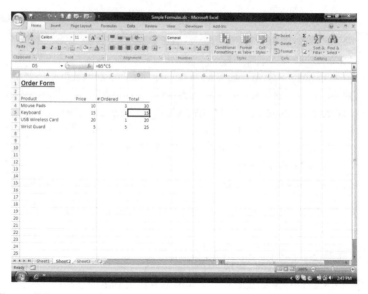

Figure 7.2
Viewing your formulas.

View All Formulas within Your Worksheet

If you have a worksheet that includes lots of formulas and you want to see them quickly, you can alter your Excel options.

To do this, perform the following:

1 Select the Office Button.

2 Next, select the Excel Options button.

3 Select the Advanced options. Scroll down your options until you see the heading **Display options for this worksheet** with the name of the worksheet chosen.

4 Select the checkbox **Show formulas in cells instead of their calculated results**, as shown in Figure 7.3.

Figure 7.3
Advanced Excel Options.

Edit Formulas

To edit a formula, perform the following:

1 Select the cell that contains the formula you wish to edit.

2 Either place your cursor in the formula bar to make edits or hit F2 (which will take you to the end of the cells formula).

3 Use standard editing techniques to change the formula. Or you can delete the formula if you like.

4 Select Enter when you have finished editing the formula.

→ Use Name Ranges within Your Formulas

We've considered the more simplistic approach to formulas so far. However, you can use name ranges to make it easier for anyone who is reading your worksheet to understand how your formula is designed to work.

Chapter 3 explained how you select and name a range. To see how those named ranges might help you with formulas, consider the following example:

=QuantitySold*UnitPrice

In this case, rather than using a cell address or a range of cell addresses, we have named these "Quantity Sold" and "Unit Price" and then created a formula using the named range. Excel will understand which cell addresses you are referencing and other readers of the spreadsheet will easily see the way the formula was put together.

Important

One interesting feature of named ranges is that you can take a cell or cell range and name it with more than one name. So you can use one name for one formula and another for a different formula. The data itself is the same, but having two different names associated with it will give you more flexibility in how you use these names in your formulas.

8

Using Basic Excel Functions

In this lesson you will learn the basics of using Excel functions within your spreadsheets. Functions go beyond formulas in that they provide a more robust method for manipulating data. But functions can be complicated at times, so we are going to get you started with some of the more common, and easy to use functions...you will build from there.

→ What is a Function?

A function is a specific type of predesigned formula that performs a specific operation on a range of data. All functions consist of two things, the function name (for example, SUM) and the arguments, which can be made up of specific numbers, cell addresses or ranges of cell addresses. You can even supply as an argument another formula or function so long as the result of that formula provides a valid argument in the function you are working with. Sometimes you may want to provide more than one argument and you can do this by using a comma.

As an example, consider the following formula:

=SUM(A1:A7,B6)

This formula includes the SUM function name (which will add the values of the data provided by the argument) with a cell range of A1 to A7 and then an additional cell address of B6 (which is included after a comma).

→ Insert a Function

There are hundreds of functions to choose from. To insert a function into your workbook you can type it in manually (much like you would with a simple formula) or you can use the **Insert Function** button which will take you through a series of dialogue boxes to fill in your arguments. As you become more proficient in the use of functions and their arguments you will be able to type them in manually; however, when getting started you will find the **Insert Function** option the more comfortable choice.

Important

There are two locations for the **Insert Function** button. One is next to your formula bar at all times and has an *fx* on it. The other is located on the Formulas ribbon, under the Function Library grouping.

To insert a simple function, perform the following:

1 Select a cell for the formula. (Note: This example has data in cells A1 through A5 and we are going to use the SUM function to place the total of those cells in A6.)

2 Type an equals sign (=) to start the formula. (This is optional.)

3 Select the Formulas ribbon. Under the Function Library grouping, select the Insert Function button.

4 The Insert Function dialogue box will appear (shown in Figure 8.1).

5 From within the Insert Function dialog you can do the following:

- *Search for a function*: Type in a brief description of what you are looking to do, then select Go.

- *Select a category*: There are many different categories to choose from to narrow down your search for the function you need (for example, Most Recently Used will show you formulas you have used in the recent past).

- *Select a function*: Once you have chosen a category you will be offered a menu of functions. For each function you select, a brief description will be provided along with possible arguments.

- *Help on this function*: This provides additional information on how to use a particular function properly.

6 Under the category **Most Recently Used**, select the SUM function.

7 The Function Arguments dialogue will appear, shown in Figure 8.2. Notice the option to insert Number1. Here you can type in your cell addresses (a cell or cell range) or you can select those cells on the worksheet and they will be added to the argument.

8 Next, you can include a secondary number in the argument if you choose. If you add a secondary number, you will then be presented with the possibility of adding a third number (and so on).

9 Notice that you have a **Formula result** = statement within this dialogue box.

10 Hit OK when you are done and you will see the results are located in your selected cell.

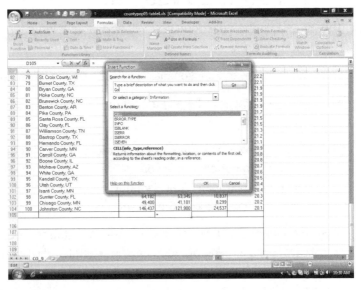

Figure 8.1
The Insert Function dialogue box.

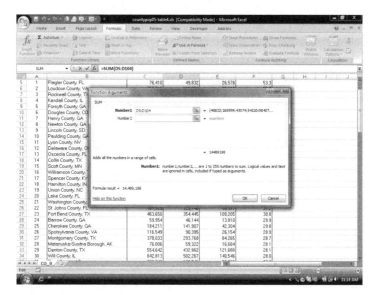

Figure 8.2
The Function Arguments dialogue box.

Timesaver tip

When trying to select the cell or cell range for the formula argument, you can select the collapse button (shown in Figure 8.3) to make the Function Arguments dialogue minimise so you can see the entire worksheet more easily. Once the arguments are selected you can select the expand button to restore the full size of the Function Arguments dialogue box.

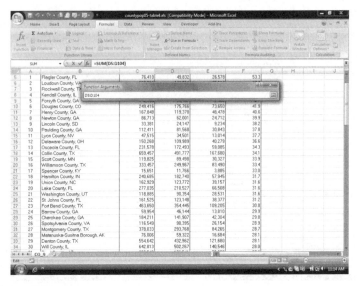

Figure 8.3
The collapse button.

→ Five Commonly Used Functions

There are five functions that you may use on a more regular basis. Along with being commonly used, they are quite easy to work with and are listed in Table 8.1.

Table 8.1 Commonly Used Functions

Function	Description	Syntax
SUM	Adds all the numbers in a range of cells	=SUM(number1, number2,...)
AVERAGE	Returns the average (arithmetic mean) of its arguments, which can be numbers or names, arrays, or references that contain numbers	=AVERAGE(number1, number2,...)
COUNT NUMBERS	Counts the number of cells in a range that contain numbers. Note: The COUNT function can be used for contiguous and non-contiguous cell ranges	=COUNT(value1, value2,...)
MAX	Returns the largest value in a set of values. Ignores logical values and text	=MAX(number1, number2,...)
MIN	Returns the smallest number in a set of values. Ignores logical values and text	=MIN(number1, number2,...)

→ Using AutoSum

Adding up the value of a group of cells (usually as a total of a row or column) is so common that Excel provides an AutoSum button to make the task even easier. When you place your cursor at the end of a row or column of numerical data that you wish to add together and press the AutoSum button (Σ ⁃), Excel will use the SUM function and attempt to automatically determine the range you want to add up based upon the location of your cursor.

To use the AutoSum, perform the following:

1 Select the cell you wish to use the SUM function in. Keep in mind that AutoSum cannot read your mind – it will either total numbers above it or to the left of it if those numbers exist. If you try to use AutoSum in a cell with no data in its column or row, AutoSum will simply insert the SUM function with no arguments.

2 You can select the AutoSum option from one of two locations:

- Off the Home ribbon, under the Editing grouping.

- Off the Formulas ribbon, under the Function Library grouping.

3 Select the AutoSum button and hit Enter.

Caveats to AutoSum

AutoSum isn't perfect. For example, if you use AutoSum with a range of cells that has empty cells, the AutoSum doesn't realise you want the entire column and chooses only the range it "believes" you want, as shown in Figure 8.4. To rectify this, just keep an eye on the range it chooses for you and edit the range accordingly.

In addition, if you try to use AutoSum at the end of a row but that cell is also the end of a column, AutoSum will total the column data by default. Again, the solution to this problem is to be aware of the range AutoSum selects for your SUM function.

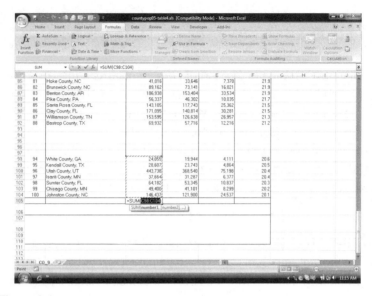

Figure 8.4
AutoSum isn't perfect.

Use the AutoSum Down Arrow

To the right of the AutoSum button is a down arrow where you can select additional functions, starting with the ones mentioned earlier in this chapter, as shown in Figure 8.5.

From the AutoSum options, along with the fab five of functions, you can select the More Functions option and it will take you to the Insert Function dialogue box.

→ Status Bar Function Results

Along the bottom of your Excel worksheet, beneath the worksheet tabs and the horizontal scroll bar, is an area called the status bar. This area can include a great deal of information. If you right-click the status bar you will see the Customize Status Bar options, shown in Figure 8.6.

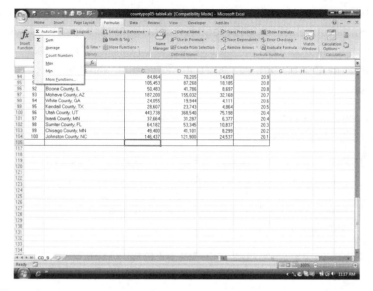

Figure 8.5
Use AutoSum's additional options.

Figure 8.6
Selecting status bar options.

There are six function options: Average, Count (which counts the number of selected cells that have data, both text or numerical), Numerical Count (which counts only the number of cells that have numerical data, as shown in Figure 8.7), Minimum, Maximum and Sum.

To use the status bar to see fast calculations of your data, perform the following:

1 First, right-click the status bar and select the types of calculations you want displayed.

2 Then, select a range of data you want analysed and calculated.

3 Notice the status bar reports your results (as shown in Figure 8.7).

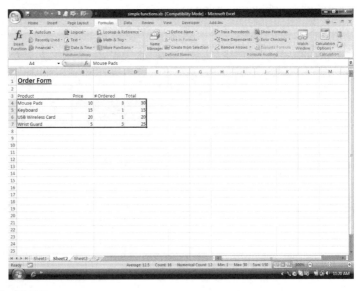

Figure 8.7
Using the status bar to show quick calculations.

9

Understanding Excel Function Groups

In this lesson you will see an overview of all the Excel function groups, including financial, logical, text, date & time, lookup, math, trig and more. This lesson isn't meant to scare you, just to show you the power you have at your fingertips with Excel 2007. Over time you will become more familiar and comfortable with many of these functions...while others you may never need at all.

→ The Function Library

To make your search for new functions easier they have been broken up into function groups. While it is impossible to discuss each and every function within this book, we can help you to see the value of each group and what types of functions you'll find within that group.

One of the first groups you might notice after the AutoSum option is the **Recently Used** option. This shows you the functions you used recently and can help you to work faster because it keeps those functions in a quick-access list.

Timesaver tip

You can learn more about any one of these functions by using the Insert Function dialogue and selecting the function and then the hyperlink **Help on this function**. You could also use the Help files to learn more about any of the functions Excel has to offer.

→ Financial Functions

There are over 50 different financial functions that can help you do everything from figuring out your mortgage payments (using the PMT function) to figuring out the bond-equivalent yield for a U.S. Treasury bill (using the TBILLEQ function).

Some of these functions are pretty advanced (like those that calculate depreciation schedules) and only benefit those who have accounting experience. Others of a more general nature can help you with loans and investments. For example, FV can help you calculate the future value of a payment. IPMT can return the interest payment for an investment based upon an interest rate and a constant payment schedule.

Financial Arguments

Some of these financial functions (and others of a similar nature) will require arguments that you've never seen before. For example:

■ *Future value (fv)*: This is the amount an investment will be worth after payments.

■ *Number of periods (nper)*: This is the total number of payments or periods for an investment. For example, for a 30-year mortgage, the nper would be 360 (which is 30 years multiplied by 12 months).

■ *Payment (pmt)*: This is the amount paid periodically towards a loan or investment (usually includes both principal and interest).

■ *Present value (pv)*: This is the value of an investment or loan at the beginning of the investment period. If you are the borrower, the pv is the amount borrowed.

■ *Rate (rate)*: This is the interest rate or discount rate for a loan or investment.

An example of a financial function (PMT(rate,nper,pv,fv,type)) with its arguments included is:

=PMT(.0825/12,360,180000)

This will determine the monthly payment of a 30-year loan at an interest rate of 8.25% a year for a loan of £180,000.

→ Logical Functions

There are seven logical functions that allow you to perform comparison functions. For example, a very important logical function is IF:

=IF(logical_test,value_if_true,value_if_false)

Note: The value_if_false portion is optional. You could specify only a True portion if you like.

The IF function will apply itself to a specific test and then will perform either a True or False formula. For example, let's say you want to look at a cell and see whether the value of that cell is greater than 100. If it is, you want to multiply the value by 10; if the value is less than 100, you want to divide the value by 10. To perform this you would type the following:

=IF(A1>100,A1*10,100/A1)

Using the other logical functions you could perform even more complicated IF calculations. For example, you could use the AND function nested within your IF to determine whether A1 is greater than 100 and less than 200, then perform the following True/False calculations. You could also use the OR function nested within your IF to determine whether A1 is greater than 100 or whether A2 is greater than 100, and so on. Your options are extensive using these comparison functions.

Important

There are information functions that you can include with your IF functions to help control your calculations. For example, you have the ISNUMBER, ISTEXT, ISERROR functions. These can be used with your IF function to rule out mistakes. Here is an example:

=IF(ISNUMBER(A1),IF(OR(A2>100,A3>100),A1*10,10/A1),"")

This looks at A1 and if there is a number in the cell then it will move on to the next IF statement. If it looks at A1 and there is no number then it will go to the False part of the statement "" and will return empty text.

→ Text Functions

Although you may think of functions as relating only to numbers, you can also use functions to manipulate text. For example, imagine a list of names in a column that includes both first name and last name. If you want to split that column so that you have a column that has all first names and a column that has all last names, you could manually separate the two. Or you can use text functions to split text values into multiple cells (or combine text from multiple cells into a single cell).

You can use UPPER, LOWER and PROPER to change text in a cell to uppercase, lowercase or sentence case (which is where the first letter of each word is capitalised).

The most popular of the text functions are LEFT, MID and RIGHT, which can be used to extract text based upon the number of characters you specify, or based upon stopping points, like a space character.

For example, if A1 has a name in it, "Lillianna Rose", and you want to extract the first name into another cell, you can type the following:

=LEFT(A1,FIND(" ",A1))

This will start at the left of your text until the point where a space is found and return the characters from the left until the space (the first name).

Important

To combine the text of two different cells you can use the CONCATENATE function but using an & (ampersand) is easier.

For example: =A1&" "&A2

This will combine the text in A1 with the text in A2 with a space in-between.

→ Date and Time Functions

These functions can be used to display the current date (using the TODAY or NOW functions) or the day of the week for any given date.

For a simple example of Date and Time, perform the following:

1 Select an empty cell to insert the function into.

2 From the Formulas ribbon, under the Function Library grouping, select the Date and Time down arrow and choose the NOW function.

3 Then select the OK button.

→ Lookup and Reference Functions

These functions are used to work with lists and tables to locate information and return it to you. These functions are designed for table interrogation. For example, the HLOOKUP and VLOOKUP functions will search through a table (horizontally or vertically).

In Figure 9.1 you see a table that contains a variety of data.

Let's say you wanted to search for a person within the table whose name you knew but you wanted to know their age. You could use a lookup formula like the following:

=VLOOKUP("Jennette",A2:C7,3,FALSE)

The first argument is the key to locating your data. The range could have also been named and then you could have used the name rather than the range. The third argument provides the column to search in. The fourth argument is an optional one.

The HLOOKUP function works the same way but for a table that is designed with data from left to right rather than up and down.

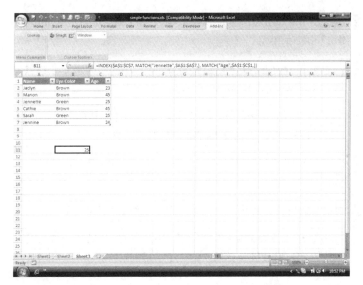

Figure 9.1
The Lookup Wizard provides a complex formula, adding to our appreciation for this tool.

The Lookup Wizard

Due to the complexity of the syntax for these functions you may want to use the Lookup Wizard to assist you. This is an Excel add-in that you have to install.

To install the Lookup Wizard Add-in, perform the following:

1 Select the Office Button; go to Excel Options, to the Add-Ins group.

2 Under the Manage options, select Go. Excel will open the Add-Ins dialogue box.

3 Select the Lookup Wizard checkbox and hit OK.

Once you have the wizard installed you go to the Add-Ins ribbon to see the Lookup menu command that has been added. To run the wizard, perform the following:

1 Select the cell range you wish to use the wizard on, including the header row.

2 Go to the Add-Ins ribbon and select the Lookup button to start the wizard, as shown in Figure 9.2.

3 First, you will verify the selection of the list. If the cell locations for your table are correct, hit Next.

4 Select the column to search in and the specific value to search for as the key. Hit Next.

5 Then, determine the format for the results. Hit Next.

6 Finally, you can type or select the cell where you wish the results to be displayed. Then hit Finish. Notice in Figure 9.3 that the formula created is actually much more complex than the one we used earlier to find the same data. The complexity may be unnecessary for our small data table but will be warranted when trying to find information in a larger data table.

Figure 9.2
Using the Lookup Wizard.

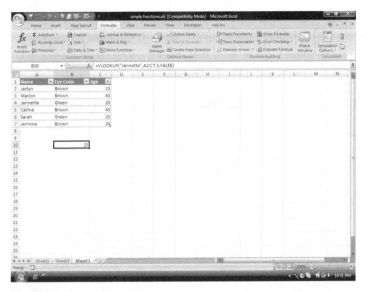

Figure 9.3
A table with data that you may want to reference.

→ Maths and Trig Functions

There are more than 60 mathematical functions that cover a wide range of subjects. Some may seem familiar from those difficult trigonometry school days (like SIN, COS and TAN for sine, cosine and tangent functions) or geometry days with PI (for 3.14xxxxx etc.) to help us determine various formulas that involve circles or spheres.

You can use the ROUND formula to round off a number into a value you prefer to see. For example, if you have a number like 873.32935540 in cell F10, you can use =ROUND(F10,3) to shorten the number down to 873.329. However, keep in mind that the number in the original cell hasn't changed, it has just been altered by the formula in the cell you have selected.

An interesting function within this group is the SUMIF function. You can use this to total a range of numbers (much like the SUM function) but only those that meet a specific requirement set that you provide. The syntax is SUMIF(range,criteria,sum_range).

So, if you consider the table in Figure 9.4, you'll notice that it is a table of 20 years of Masters Tournaments. Let's say you wanted to add up all Tiger Woods' scores for all the times he won. You could use the following formula: =SUMIF(B2:B22,"Tiger Woods",C2:C22).

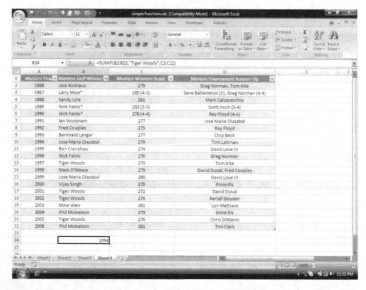

Figure 9.4
Using the SUMIF function.

→ Additional Functions

Along with the functions we have considered, there are more functions to work with, including the following:

- Statistical

- Engineering

- Cube

- Information

Some of the functions within these groups are repeated from other groupings because they apply in more than one forum.

10

Troubleshoot Function Errors

In this lesson you will learn how to troubleshoot errors that occur at times when working with functions. When an error occurs you usually receive a cryptic looking code in your Excel worksheet and you will learn how to use that code to determine the problem. In addition, you will learn how to evaluate your formulas and work with error-checking tools.

→ Identifying Errors

Because of the complexity of some of the formulas and functions within Excel you will find at times that your functions will return errors. There are seven error codes you might see and, depending on the cause of the error, you will either need to revise your formula or change the arguments to reflect a new cell range.

When you receive an error message the cell will also be flagged with a little green triangle in the upper left-hand corner. If you select the cell you will be shown a smart tag that will offer you information on the cause of the problem and possible solutions, as shown in Figure 10.1.

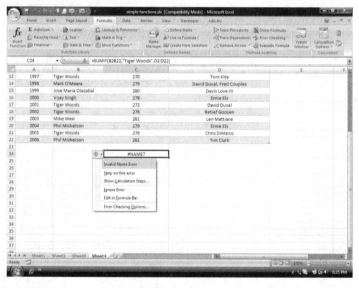

Figure 10.1
A smart tag can help you fix your formula error.

→ Common Formula Error Codes

Table 10.1 shows the seven common error codes you may encounter within your Excel worksheet. You'll notice that all error messages begin with a #.

→ Automated Error Correction

10

There are times when you have to manually evaluate why a formula isn't working. However, Excel includes several tools to help resolve your errors.

Formula AutoCorrect

When you are adding a formula into your cells, if you try to use incorrect syntax the Formula AutoCorrect will kick in and will not allow you to proceed without correcting the problem. Formula AutoCorrect will even offer to solve the problem for you.

Consider Figure 10.2, where we are trying to force Excel to ignore an incorrect syntax error for a VLOOKUP function. Excel refuses to allow us to ignore the error and continues to prompt that we accept its solution or fix the error personally.

Table 10.1 Common Error Codes

Error Code	Reason for Error	Possible Solutions
#DIV/0!	Formula is trying to divide by a zero or a blank cell	Check the formula's arguments to ensure it is not referring to a blank cell
#N/A	Formula doesn't have a valid value for the argument	Check your formula for problems with Lookup arguments
#NAME?	Formula contains text that is not a valid function	You may have misspelled a function or a range name. You also could have included text in your arguments and failed to use "" to indicate your text
#NULL!	Occurs when you reference two areas that don't intersect	It's possible you are trying to calculate a formula with column and row labels that do not have common cells. Review your formula and choose new labels with cells in common
NUM!	The value is too large, too small, imaginary or not found	Excel is designed to handle incredibly large and small numbers, so this error indicates that you may have used a function incorrectly
#REF!	Formula contains a reference that is invalid	This can occur when changes are made in your worksheet to cells referenced by a formula. Check the formula references to see which cell addresses are no longer valid
#VALUE!	Formula contains an argument that is of the wrong type	This occurs when a formula is mixed with numbers and text incorrectly. For example, if you try to add text with a number

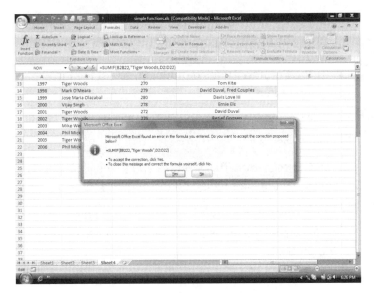

Figure 10.2
AutoCorrect detects syntax errors and tries to assist you.

AutoCorrect is not designed to perform advanced formula diagnostics. It focuses on syntax errors such as missing quotation marks or unmatched parentheses. It can detect errors that relate to reversed cell references (for example, you type 7B accidentally when you mean B7). AutoCorrect can also detect accidental spaces in your formula, extra operators (like an extra = sign), additional or incorrect range identifiers (for example, a semicolon (;) when a colon (:) is required) and these types of syntax problems in your formulas.

Formula Auditing

On the Formulas ribbon is a grouping called Formula Auditing which holds some very important tools you can use in clearing up any problems you are having with the formulas in your worksheet.

To manually check for errors in your worksheet you can use the Error Checking button. Your worksheet may have more than one error, so when you run the Error Checking tool it will start the process with the first error of the current sheet, as shown in Figure 10.3.

To use the Error Checking button, perform the following:

1 Select the Formulas ribbon.

2 Under the Formula Auditing grouping, select the Error Checking button.

3 You will be presented with a number of options, shown in Figure 10.3:

■ *Help on this error*: This will take you to the Help files to provide more information on the particular type of error.

■ *Show Calculation Steps*: This will step you through each operation and help you track down the source of the problem.

■ *Ignore Error*: If the error is minor and doesn't concern you, or if you know what to do to fix it, you can ignore it.

■ *Edit in Formula Bar*: For simple errors that can be corrected easily, you can select this option to allow you to edit the formula before changing the Error Checking dialogue box.

■ *Previous/Next*: These buttons will help you walk through your worksheet fixing all the errors within your formulas.

4 Once you have fixed the errors to the extent you are comfortable, hit the red X button to close the dialogue box.

Important

When you select the Ignore option to ignore an error, this gets saved within your worksheet. Even if you send it to others, that error will remain ignored. To reset this setting for your workbook, or for a workbook you have inherited from someone else, select the Options button from the Error Checking dialogue box. From within your Options, shown in Figure 10.4, select the Reset Ignored Errors button.

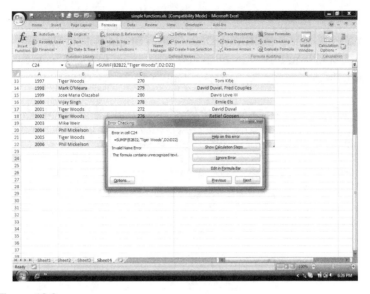

Figure 10.3
Using the Error Checking tools.

Figure 10.4
Reset Ignored Errors button.

Evaluate Your Formula

When you select the **Show Calculation Steps** option from the
Error Checking tool, you will actually be taken to the Evaluate
Formula dialogue box, shown in Figure 10.5.

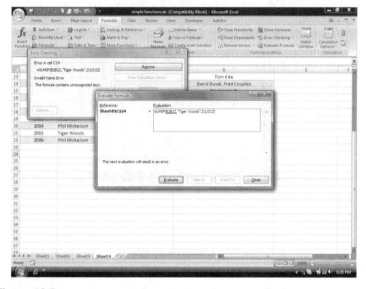

Figure 10.5
The Evaluate Formula dialogue box.

You can click the Evaluate button to step through the formula until
you reach the cause of the error. The Step In and Step Out buttons
allow you to look into formulas that refer to other formulas in other
cells to see whether these are the cause of your problem.

Additional Auditing Tools

If you look at the Formula Auditing grouping you will see a few
options that may assist further in reviewing the various formulas
you are using on your worksheet.

■ *Trace Precedents*: Shows arrows that indicate which cells
affect the value of the currently selected cell.

■ *Trace Dependents*: Shows arrows that indicate which cells are
affected by the value of the currently selected cell.

- *Remove Arrows*: Removes the arrows drawn by the Trace Precedents and/or Trace Dependents options.

- *Show Formulas*: Provides a quick way to see the formulas in your cells instead of the results.

Figure 10.6 shows you how these auditing tools provide an easier way to audit your worksheet formulas.

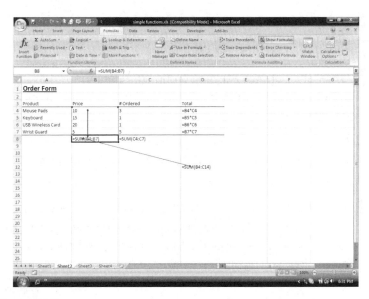

Figure 10.6
The Trace Dependents/Precedents options and the Show Formulas option from the Formula Auditing grouping.

→ Using the Watch Window

In more complicated Excel workbooks you might have cells referencing other cells in different worksheets. As you work on your data, values will change and formulas will update. If you are working on one worksheet then it's easy to see the changes; however, when you are working across multiple sheets (or even multiple workbooks) this can become difficult to track.

The Watch Window options, located on the Formulas ribbon under the Formula Auditing grouping, can help you track formula results by giving you a floating window to which you can add cells you want to track. With Watch Window you won't have to switch back and forth between your worksheets (or workbooks) to audit how changes affect your data.

To use the Watch Window, perform the following:

1 First, select a cell you want to watch.

2 Select the Formulas ribbon.

3 Under the Formula Auditing grouping, select the Watch Window button, which brings up the floating Watch Window dialogue.

4 For additional cells to watch, select the Add Watch button and either type in or select the cell (or cells) you want to watch, as shown in Figure 10.7.

5 Keep the floating window open so you can monitor those cells in real time. However, if you choose to close the window (using the X in the upper right-hand corner) and open it again, your settings will remain.

Important

You can make the size of the floating window larger or smaller by selecting the box's side handles and dragging them. You can also select column headings if you want to sort the columns, or resize the columns by placing your cursor in-between the column headings and dragging the line in one direction or another.

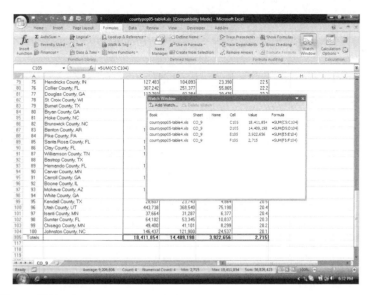

Figure 10.7
Working with the Watch Window options.

Timesaver tip

You can use named ranges in the Watch Window to make your tracking much easier to understand at a glance. There is a Name column where the Watch Window will display the name of your selected cell, so you know quickly what you are looking at.

→ Formula Error Checking Options

In the options of your Excel workbook you can alter the way error checking is performed. We considered this above with the option to Reset Ignored Errors; however, this section will discuss some of the other options found on the Formulas page (shown again in Figure 10.8 for easy reference).

Figure 10.8
Excel Options, under the Formulas group, allows you to control how your error checking works.

Let's consider the options in two tables: Error Checking (Table 10.2) and Error Checking Rules (Table 10.3).

Table 10.2 Error Checking Options

Option	Description
Enable background error checking	To turn automatic error checking on or off, select this checkbox
Indicate errors using this colour	The default colour is a green triangle in the upper left-hand corner of a cell. You can change the colour to whatever you like
Reset Ignored Errors	Mentioned earlier, this button will reset the error counter to include errors that you have (or another person has) chosen to ignore

Table 10.3 Error Checking Rules Options

Option	Description
Cells containing formulas that result in an error	Searches formulas for the correct syntax, arguments and data types. If an error is found, one of the seven standard error messages is returned
Inconsistent calculated column formula in tables	There is a variety of reasons why a calculated column formula might be inconsistent, but this setting will help to flag the inconsistency and then you can use the Error Checking tools to track down the cause of the problem
Cells containing years represented as two digits	The cell may contain a two-digit year date that can be misinterpreted in a formula. For example, if the cell contains a date that is entered as 01/01/10, the application could misunderstand the date. Is it for the year 1910 or 2010? This setting will check for these types of problems
Numbers formatted as text or preceded by an apostrophe	Either accidentally, or by copying from other locations, your numbers are formatted as text (which interferes with your formulas). This option will help you find these types of issues
Formulas inconsistent with other formulas in the region	This setting highlights inconsistencies seen between formulas in the same region. For example, if several formulas use the SUM function to add together a consistent range (for example, SUM(A1:C1), SUM(A2:C2) and so forth) and then you have a formula like SUM(B3–F4), this would be red flagged as an inconsistency
Formulas which omit cells in a region	Spots strange omissions in a formula range. For example, imagine you had data in cells A1, B1 and C1. You used the SUM function to add this data with the range A1:C1. Then you expanded your data to include D1, E1 and F1. If your SUM function was never updated to include the new range A1:F1, your error checking will red flag this as a possible need to update your formula
Unlocked cells containing formulas	Alerts you that a cell containing a formula is not protected from being altered
Formulas referring to empty cells	When you have a cell that is contained in a formula range that is blank, this may cause results you didn't intend. This will flag empty cells and you can decide whether you want to leave them empty or place a 0 in the cell to have the cell count in your formulas
Data entered in a table is invalid	Indicates when data is invalid in a table. You can locate and correct such invalid data by using the Data Validation button from the Data ribbon, under the Data Tools grouping

10

11

Using Tables to Sort and Filter Data

In this lesson you will learn how to work with your data in tables. By working with your data in an organised table format you have the ability to sort and manipulate that data to quickly show you what you need to see at any given time, without hurting the data itself. This chapter will show you how to sort and filter your data.

→ Sorting Your Data

In previous chapters we have discussed how to create an official Excel table (using the Home ribbon, under the Styles grouping, and selecting the Format As Table). This selection does more than simply format your tables to make them more professional looking and easy to follow for presentations. You may have noticed upon using this formatting option that the top of your table is changed somewhat to allow you to sort your data based upon a variety of predefined filters.

Excel will look to the first row of your table for column labels as a means of identifying each column of the data that you will be sorting. It's recommended that you use column labels, however it's not required. In the event you do not use column labels, Excel will apply a standard set of headers (i.e. Column1, Column2 and so forth), as shown in Figure 11.1.

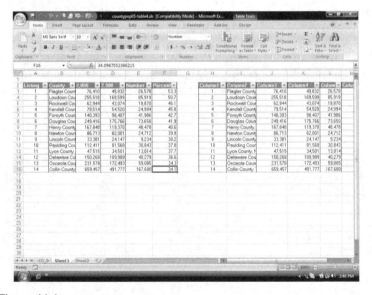

Figure 11.1
Here you can see two tables, one that has column labels and one that doesn't so it gets the generic labels.

Important

Your data doesn't have to be in a table to be sorted. You can use the sorting options for data entered within your worksheet that hasn't been formatted as a table.

Ascending/Descending Data Sorts (Using Sort & Filter)

To quickly sort your data (either in a table or not), perform the following:

1 First, select a cell in the column you want to have the data sorted by.

2 Select the Home ribbon and under the Editing grouping select the Sort & Filter button. Note: You can also select the Data ribbon and use the Sort & Filter grouping to find these same tools.

3 Choose to **Sort A to Z** (the ascending sort, which includes numbers going from 0–9) or **Sort Z to A** (the descending sort, which includes numbers going from 9–0). Note: If you choose a column that is made up of numbers, then the options you will be shown are **Sort Smallest to Largest** and **Sort Largest to Smallest**.

11

Jargon buster

Sorting data doesn't mean disrupting one column's data and leaving the corresponding data in the current order. When you decide to sort a column and data in that column is shifted according to the sort specifications, the surrounding data is moved too. So you never have to worry that it's going to jumble your data.

Sorting Data Using Table Column Headers

Although you can use the Sort & Filter options to sort data either
in a table or not, an easier way is to use the column header
down arrows. To sort data using the table column headers,
perform the following:

1 First, select the down arrow for the column you wish to sort
your data by, as shown in Figure 11.2.

2 Choose to **Sort A to Z** (the ascending sort, which includes
numbers going from 0–9) or **Sort Z to A** (the descending sort,
which includes numbers going from 9–0). Note: If you choose
a column that is made up of numbers, then the options you
will be shown are **Sort Smallest to Largest** and **Sort
Largest to Smallest**.

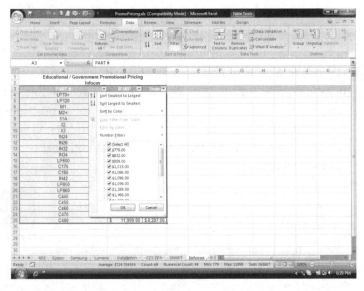

Figure 11.2
Sorting data within your table using column headings.

→ Performing Custom Sorts

Excel offers you the ability to sort data in a column by more than the values within the cells. You can sort your data based upon font colour, cell colour, icons and so forth. You can also sort by multiple columns using different criteria.

To create a custom sort of your data, perform the following:

1 First, place your cursor within the table you wish to perform the sort for.

2 Then, there are several ways to select the custom sort options, including the following:

■ In a table, select the down arrow at the top of any of the column headings. Select **Sort by Colour** and then **Custom Sort**. This will bring up the Sort dialogue box.

■ On the Home ribbon, under the Editing grouping, select the Sort & Filter button and then choose **Custom Sort**. This will bring up the Sort dialogue box.

■ On the Data ribbon, under the Sort & Filter grouping, select the Sort button. This will bring up the Sort dialogue box.

3 From the Sort dialogue box (shown in Figure 11.3) you can see that you have the ability to choose the following:

■ *Column – Sort by*: Lets you choose from the headings of your table. If you don't have headings then you can sort by the generic column headings. If you are working with data simply input into your worksheet without being formatted as a table, you can choose Excel column headings (i.e. A, B, C and so forth).

■ *Sort On – Values, Cell Colour, Font Colour, Cell Icon*: These options not only allow you to customise your sort by values, but also by colours and icons (that you may have included with conditional formatting).

11

■ *Order*: Depending on what you are sorting, you can determine ascending or descending, top or bottom orders for your sort.

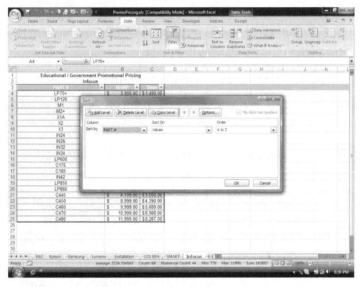

Figure 11.3
Performing a custom sort using the Sort dialogue box.

Sort by Multiple Columns

Excel has the ability to sort multiple columns in sequence. In other words, if you have several columns of data (shown in Figure 11.4) and you want the final sort to have your Orders from largest to smallest, but your Sales People in alphabetical order as well, you would perform the following:

1 Starting with the Sales People column, use the sorting options to sort in ascending order.

2 Then, sort the second column, the Orders column, by ascending order.

3 Notice that your second column is given the higher precedence and the numbers are in ascending order, however your Sales People (although appearing jumbled) are listed alphabetically within each section.

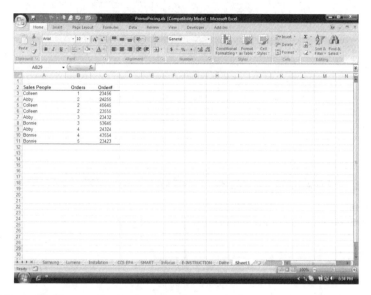

Figure 11.4
Sorting multiple columns in sequence.

Another, more controlled way to perform the same sort is to use the Sort dialogue box. You can tell Excel to sort by more than one column. To do this, open your Sort dialogue and perform the following:

1 Starting with the Sales People column, use the sorting options to sort in ascending order.

2 Then, select the Add Level button, which will add another column to sort by, as shown in Figure 11.5.

3 Select the Order column, sort on values, in the A to Z order.

4 Hit OK and notice that the results are the same as earlier where the Order column is given primary concern but the Sales People are in A to Z order where possible.

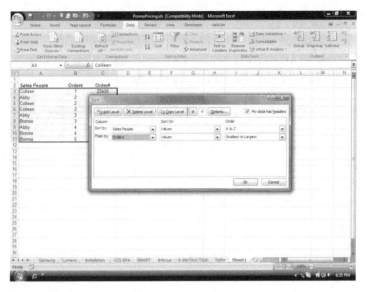

Figure 11.5
Sorting multiple columns using the Sort dialogue.

Sort by Day of the Week or Month

If you need to sort a column by days of the week or months, you realise that sorting these alphabetically would be a problem because it would completely change around the order for days and months.

There are four default options when attempting to sort by dates. To use these, perform the following:

1 From within the Sort dialogue box, select the column of days or months you wish to sort.

2 Select the Order options down arrow and select the **Custom List** option. This will bring up the Custom Lists dialogue box, shown in Figure 11.6.

3 From here you can select one of four predesigned lists for both full names and abbreviations of the week days or months.

4 Or you can type your own list in the **List entries** portion to create custom lists for sorting your data.

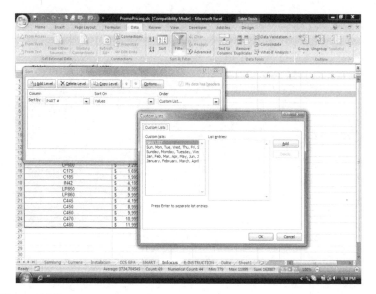

Figure 11.6
Creating custom sorting lists for days of the week, months, or your own invention.

→ Filter Your Data

Filtering your data is different from sorting. Sorting takes the entire table and puts it in an order based upon specific criteria that you have selected. Filtering actually eliminates from your view (or filters out of sight) portions that do not meet the criteria you have selected.

The easiest way to filter your data is through the automatic filtering options that Excel provides. You can see these in one of two ways, either because you have taken a cell range and formatted it to be a table (and then you will notice the down arrows at the top of your column headers), or, if you are working with information that you haven't explicitly defined as a table, by putting your cursor in a cell with data, going to the Data ribbon and selecting the Filter button, shown in Figure 11.7. Notice in the figure that one table has filtering on and the other has it turned off.

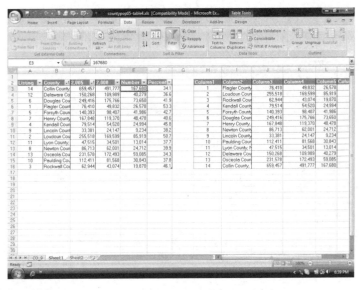

Figure 11.7
The Filter button turns filtering on and off for your tables.

Important

In tables that you have formatted as such, the automatic filtering options appear in the headers (or generic headers will be created if you don't have them already). However, you can turn these off by placing your cursor in the table and de-selecting the Filter button.

To use the automatic filter, perform the following:

1 Select the down arrow next to one of your table column headings. Choose the column that you want to use as the basis for your filtering.

2 There are different types of filters to choose from depending on the column data:

■ If you are filtering text, you can select the **Text Filters** and choose one of the text filter options (shown in Figure 11.8).

- If you are filtering numbers, you can select the **Number Filters** and choose one of the number filter options (shown in Figure 11.9).

3 You can define many different criteria for your text filter (for example, equals, does not equal, contains, does not contain, etc.). You can define many different criteria for your numeric filter as well (for example, equals, greater than, Top 10, etc.).

4 You can also define a custom filter that allows you to select more than one filter type and criterion.

5 Notice that Excel will change the look of your column headings to show a little funnel that indicates you have a filter established on that particular column. This will make it easier later on if you need to remove filters for you to remember which columns have filters established on them.

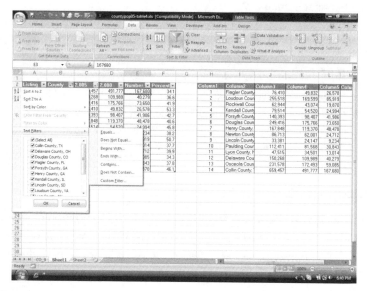

Figure 11.8
Text filter settings.

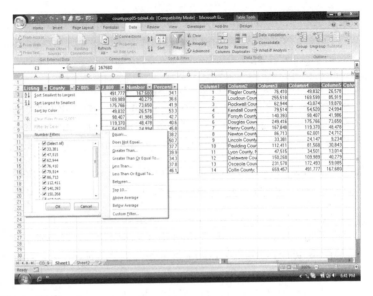

Figure 11.9
Number filter settings.

Custom Filters

In filtering your data you can select a custom filter option (shown in Figure 11.10), noted above in the step-by-step process of using filters. You can choose two different types of filters using either an AND or OR operator to increase the functionality of your filter.

If you want to strictly see two different criteria, select the AND option. If you want to see one or the other criterion, select the OR option.

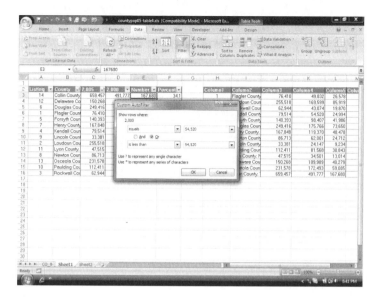

Figure 11.10
Creating a custom filter.

Important

You'll note that you can only create a custom filter that allows for two criteria. You can circumvent this supposed limitation by making a copy of the column you are filtering by and establishing additional sets of criteria for that column. Then, one set of filtering criteria will apply to one column and narrow down your options and the second set will narrow down the copied column.

12

Creating Pivot Tables

In this lesson you will learn how to create pivot tables. These are special methods of manipulating your data so that you can extract it from long lists of data without using special formulas or functions. We will show you how to use one of Excel's most powerful features… Pivot Tables.

→ Understanding Pivot Tables

Because they seem so intimidating, many people avoid pivot tables, one of the most powerful features in Excel. Pivot tables can, in fact, be complicated. But that doesn't always have to be the case and in actuality you can get started with simple pivot tables and work your way up.

Jargon buster

A **pivot table** helps you extract information from a long list, without formulas or functions. You begin with a table, choose columns and rows to snap in, and you end up with an easy-to-read report.

As an example of what a pivot table looks like and how they are created, consider Figure 12.1. This figure shows a simple list of items purchased by different individuals on different days. Obviously there are many ways to analyse this data, but let's say your entire goal is to see what the total was for each person along with how many items each purchased. Now you have the list of data and it wouldn't take you too long to perform this manually, but imagine the list is much larger. The pivot table helps you quickly restructure the data.

→ Create a Simple Pivot Table

For you to see how a pivot table is created we will begin with a simple table that is filled with data about student grades, months that exams were taken, by which students and their grade for that exam, as shown in Figure 12.2. You can create your own in a worksheet to practise with.

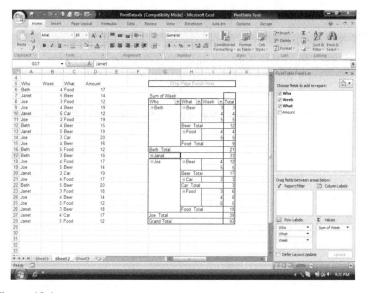

Figure 12.1
A simple pivot table offers immediate benefits.

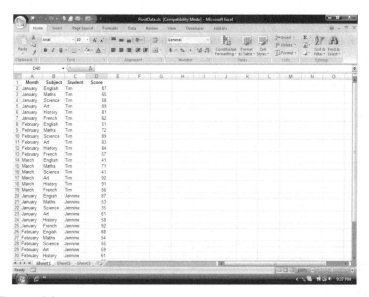

Figure 12.2
A basic list of student grades.

To turn that list into a simple pivot table, perform the following:

1 To begin, go to the Insert ribbon, under the Tables grouping, select the Pivot Table option. The **Create PivotTable** dialogue box appears, as shown in Figure 12.3.

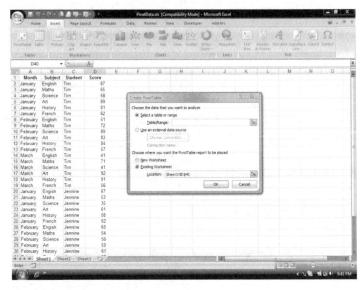

Figure 12.3
The Create PivotTable dialogue box.

2 You are asked to select a range. Select the data in your simple table.

3 You can choose to create the pivot table in a new worksheet or on the current worksheet. That is your choice, although for this example we will keep it on the current worksheet. You can then provide the location cells (although Excel will choose a location for you, but you may want to change this).

4 Select OK.

5 You will then be shown an outline for your pivot table and the PivotTable Field List, as shown in Figure 12.4.

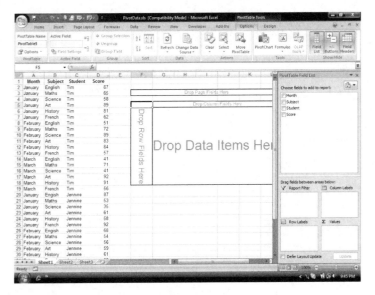

Figure 12.4
The PivotTable Field List.

6 You start to formulate the report for your data by dragging the fields to their appropriate locations on the pivot table. It may look confusing at first, but we will walk through each step and you will see it come together. To start with, move the Month field over to the Row area, as shown in Figure 12.5.

7 Now move the Subject field over to the Column area and the Score field over to the Data area. Your pivot table should look similar to the table in Figure 12.6.

8 To get your students to come into the table you can add them directly to the table by selecting the checkbox next to the Student field. However, to make the table more interesting, drag the Student field over to the Page Fields area, as shown in Figure 12.7.

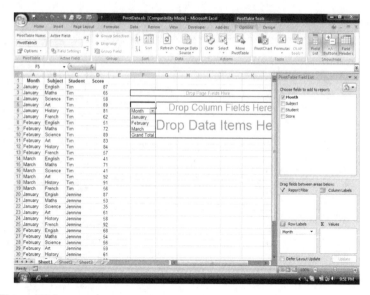

Figure 12.5
Moving items into the Row area.

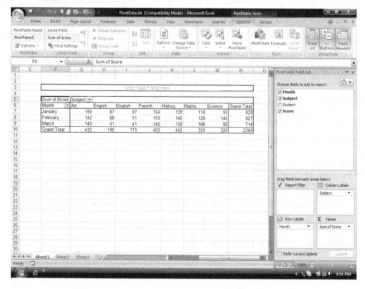

Figure 12.6
Your pivot table is shaping up.

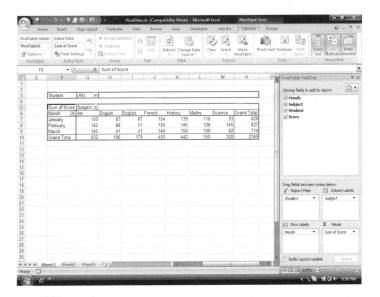

Figure 12.7
The finishing touches on your simple pivot table.

9 Before we finish these steps, consider the four areas in the PivotTable Field List. You could also have dragged the fields down to those four locations: Report Filter, Column Labels, Row Labels and Values.

10 When you have your pivot table all set, select the small x at the top right-hand corner of the PivotTable Field List to close that dialogue and then you can see how the pivot table can really be a timesaver by changing the student names to quickly see their grades for any given month.

As you have seen from the steps on creating a simple pivot table, you take the column headings (called fields in your pivot table) and place them in row and column fields to define how the table will be constructed. The data field contains the information you are looking to summarise into an easy-to-read report. The page fields area lets you refine the view by creating different pivot table views for each item in that column.

You can have multiple row and column fields and you can change the type of action you want on your data items. The default is Sum, but you can choose to average or count the values.

→ Update Your Pivot Table

Because a pivot table doesn't affect your actual data, you can create new pivot tables and switch the rows and columns around in whatever manner you choose without worrying about the original data. Whenever you create a new pivot table or alter the layout of an existing one, Excel will update the data from the original list. If any of that data has changed, Excel will update the pivot table with the changes.

However, if you add data (from our example above, let's say you add a new student's grades) or edit the data from the original table, these changes do not appear automatically in the pivot table you have created. Consider Figure 12.8 to see that we have updated the grade for one of the student's classes but the pivot table doesn't reflect this change.

You can see from the figure that you have a special Options ribbon when working in pivot tables. To update the data from your table to your pivot table, look under the Data grouping and select the Refresh button.

Important

Pivot tables are useful when you have large data tables that you need to see from differing viewpoints. They can really make your data come alive and their uses can be infinite. However, you might look to find deeper information on the use of pivot tables by searching for more information online. One excellent resource for advanced pivot table info is Joseph Rubin's **www.exceltip.com** under the Excel Pivot Tables category.

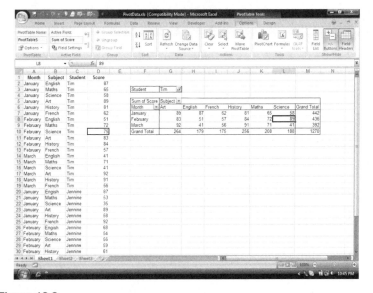

Figure 12.8

You need to manually update a pivot table if the data has been edited or added to.

12

13

Protecting Your Workbook and Worksheets

In this lesson you will learn how to protect your workbook and worksheets through password protection methods, hiding of certain cells or a locking and unlocking of cells. In addition, we will introduce you to Information Rights Management (IRM), a special method of protecting your documents.

→ Protect Your Data

Excel makes it possible to protect your data one cell at a time, or through a lockdown of the entire workbook. There are situations where you do not want people to change the data or the formulas and functions you have worked so hard to incorporate into your workbook. There are several different layers of protection you can configure. Let's begin with the most powerful.

Password Protect Your Entire Workbook

You can configure password protection on a workbook that can prevent unauthorised access (through advanced key encryption) that stops users from opening the workbook, or allows users to open it but prevents modification of the workbook.

Jargon buster

Encryption is a process of making a document unreadable. You cannot open the document without a key to decode (or decrypt) the document.

Important

Another method of securing your data is by encrypting the workbook using the Prepare tools found under the Office Button. Excel 2007 uses 128-bit AES encryption for password protection with the new Open XML formats.

To enable a password that will prevent unauthorised access of your workbook, perform the following:

1 Open the workbook you want to protect.

2 Select the Office Button and then Save As.

3 Select the Tools button and then General Options, shown in Figure 13.1, and the General Options dialogue box comes up.

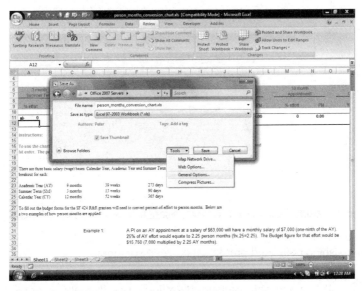

Figure 13.1
Saving your workbook with a password.

4 From the General Options dialogue box (shown in Figure 13.2), you can do one or both of the following:

■ Type a password in the **Password to open** box if you want people to use a password to view the workbook. This option uses advanced password encryption.

■ Type a password in the **Password to modify** box if you want people to use a password to modify the workbook. This option doesn't use encryption.

The **Read-only recommended** option, if selected, will prompt the user to see whether they want to open the file as read-only, which will help with the protection of the file's contents.

13

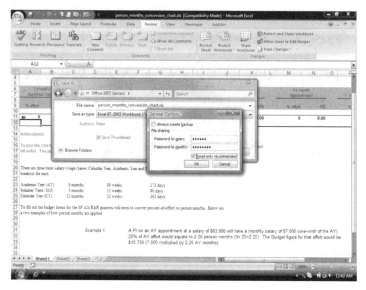

Figure 13.2
Establishing password protection on your workbook.

5 You can use both password settings (one that allows access to the workbook, the other to allow people to modify the workbook). It is recommended that you use two different passwords, one for each option. Then select OK.

6 For each of your chosen settings you will be asked to confirm your password before proceeding.

Important

When establishing a password, whether for an Excel worksheet, your computer itself, or online websites, it is very important to make your password as complex as possible, while still memorable to you. Passwords that are more complex are stronger and harder for outsiders to crack. Using lowercase characters, uppercase characters, numbers and special characters all in one password is essential to strengthen it. So, a password like banana123 is a horrible password, whereas RBalboa#6! is more effective.

Workbook Protection Settings

You can establish some additional workbook-wide protection through the Review ribbon settings. To see these settings, go to the Review ribbon, under the Changes grouping, and select the Protect Workbook button to see your options.

Select **Restrict Editing**, which will allow you to select protection of the Structure or Windows (or both) with an optional password.

- *Structure*: Prevents the user from doing things like changing the order of sheets in a workbook, adding or deleting sheets and so forth.

- *Windows*: Prevents the user from being able to resize or move the window.

→ Protect Specific Aspects of Your Workbook

In addition to protecting an entire workbook, you can protect worksheets and individual cells from being modified. Knowing the amount of work that goes into creating a good workbook, you should do your best to protect it, while allowing the proper individuals the opportunity to see and/or modify it.

13

Important

If you are concerned about your workbook being tampered with, it would be wise to make a backup copy of the file and keep this separate from the file that is put on the network servers or shared through email. The only caution we would like to give you in doing this is that you may end up with two versions of the same document and this can lead to confusion or added work as you try to merge the data into one complete document.

Lock or Unlock Cells

When you protect your worksheets, the cells within your worksheets automatically become locked. The reason for this is that they are already, by default, configured to be locked. To verify this, open a workbook, go to any worksheet and select any cell or cell range. If you go to the Home ribbon, under the Editing grouping, select the Format button. Notice under Protection that the **Lock Cell** option is highlighted. So, when you protect a worksheet, this protects those cells too. However, if you wanted to allow certain cells to be modified you would want to unlock those cells.

To unlock cells in a worksheet, perform the following:

1 On the worksheet you want to allow to be edited, select those cells by either selecting an entire range or by selecting individual cells, perhaps those cells that are responses to a form, or those cells that are part of a table you want to allow a colleague to edit. You can select individual cells by holding down the Ctrl button when you select each cell.

2 On the Home ribbon, under the Editing grouping, select the Format button.

3 De-select the **Lock Cell** option. Note: You could also go to the cell formatting dialogue, to the Protection tab and de-select the locked checkbox.

Protect Your Worksheets

Locking/unlocking cells in a worksheet is only one step in the process of protecting a worksheet. Until you actually lock the worksheet itself, those options do nothing.

To lock the worksheet, perform the following:

1 Go to the worksheet you want to protect.

2 Go to the Review ribbon, under the Changes grouping.

3 Select the Protect Sheet button and the Protect Sheet dialogue box will appear (as shown in Figure 13.3).

4 Select the options that you want to protect. For example, while you may not want an individual to be able to alter the data or delete rows and columns, you may want to allow them to alter the formatting of your worksheet.

5 Insert a password to unprotect the sheet. Note: This step is optional.

6 When you are done, select the OK button.

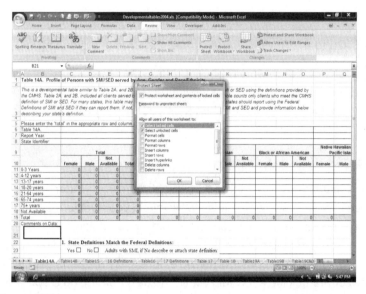

Figure 13.3
Determining which portions of your worksheet will be locked down from the Protect Sheet dialogue box.

Jargon buster

Protection is used to prevent accidental changes to your data or your worksheet formulas, but do not mistake it for security. Even though you use a password for worksheet protection, this is a very easily cracked password and there are many programs on the Internet that can be downloaded for free to break through your protection.

To unprotect a worksheet that is currently protected, perform the following:

1 Go to the worksheet you want to unprotect.

2 Go to the Review ribbon, under the Changes grouping.

3 Select the Unprotect Sheet button. The sheet will automatically unprotect itself if there is no password. If a password was established then you will be prompted for that password and once verified the sheet will be unprotected.

Hiding Cells (aka Hiding Formulas)

This feature may give some the wrong impression. After you hide a cell you will notice that it is still visible in your worksheet. This may confuse you a bit because you know you followed all the directions and hid the cell. It's important to note that hiding a cell doesn't make the contents invisible, it actually prevents the cell's true contents (like a formula within the cell) from being displayed in the formula bar.

To hide a cell, perform the following:

1 Select a cell or cell range that you wish to hide.

2 You can do one of the following: a) right-click the cells and choose **Format Cells**, or b) go to the Home ribbon, to the Editing grouping and select the Format button. Then select the **Format Cells** option.

3 Go to the Protection tab, shown in Figure 13.4.

4 Select the **Hidden** option.

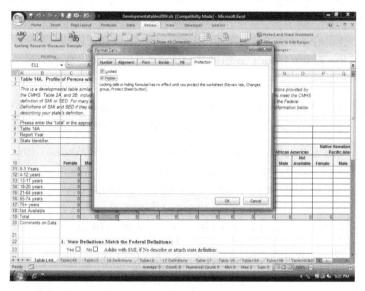

Figure 13.4
Hiding your cells' formulas.

Important

Keep in mind that the cells will not be "hidden" unless you protect the worksheet as well.

→ Additional Protection Tools

Excel gives you some tools to assist in working with your protection when on a domain. For example, you have the ability to lock down a worksheet but make a cell range available only to those who have a password, or only to those who have been excluded from being locked out.

To use the **Allow Users to Edit Ranges** tool, perform the following:

1 First, make sure your worksheet is not protected. If it is, then your **Allow Users to Edit Ranges** option will be greyed out.

2 From the Review ribbon, under the Changes grouping, select the **Allow Users to Edit Ranges** button. This will take you to the **Allow Users to Edit Ranges** dialogue box, shown in Figure 13.5.

3 Select the **New** button to configure a range (which you can type or select) and a range password (which is optional).

4 You can use the Permissions button to specify those who may edit the range without a password. Being part of an Active Directory domain will make this option easier to use because you can select users and groups within your company that you want to provide access to the range for.

5 When ranges and permissions have been established, select the OK button.

6 Remember to re-protect the worksheet.

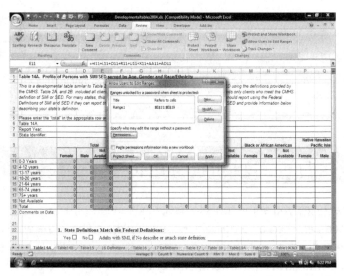

Figure 13.5
Allowing users to edit ranges.

Information Rights Management (IRM)

Using IRM you can set permissions that define who can open, edit, print, forward or copy documents. IRM works by installing a digital certificate that allows you to encrypt the document. You assign permissions based upon email addresses.

Important

To use this technology you first must install the latest Windows Rights Management client from Microsoft's website. You must also have either a network server running Windows Server 2003 with Windows Rights Management Services (and Active Directory) or a .NET password registered with Microsoft's Information Rights Management Service.

To learn more about setting up IRM in Excel 2007, begin by reading the information provided by the IRM dialogue screens. To initiate these screens, go to the Review ribbon, under the Changes grouping, and select the Protect Workbook button to see your options.

Under **Restrict Permission**, select the Restricted Access option, which will start the Service Sign-Up dialogue box, shown in Figure 13.6.

You must select **Yes** to proceed to the next set of questions. To learn more about IRM and its benefits, see the following link:

http://office.microsoft.com/en-us/help/HA010721681033.aspx

13

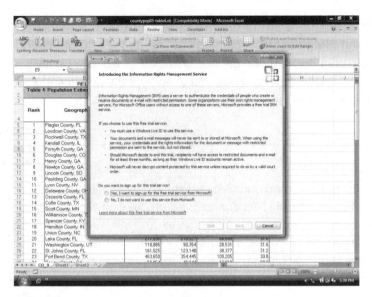

Figure 13.6
The IRM Service Sign-Up dialogue.

14

Changing the View

In this lesson you will learn how to alter the view of your workbooks and worksheets. You can work with different views of your workbook, or freeze headings as you work with larger worksheets, split the worksheet window so you see two parts of the same document and more.

→ Worksheet Views

Most new Excel users will continue to use the default view settings they see when they open Excel until they begin to feel more comfortable with the application itself. You can alter the way your data appears without affecting data or how it will print.

Making changes to the view of your worksheet may allow you to work with your data more easily, especially when dealing with large amounts of data. You can zoom in and out of your worksheet, make the view full screen, hide information, use multiple panes and more.

Changing Your Workbook Views

The view we have been working in is called Normal and it is the default view for new workbooks. To see the view you are currently in, perform the following:

1 In your workbook, select the View ribbon. Under the Workbook Views grouping you will see the Normal button is highlighted, as shown in Figure 14.1.

2 A second way of ascertaining your view is by looking down at the status bar. There are shortcuts to changing the workbook views. You'll notice that the first one, the Normal view, is highlighted.

To change your workbook view you can either select a different view from the status bar, or you can select a different view from the View ribbon under the Workbook View grouping. But it is important to know what each view does and how it may benefit you to switch at times between them.

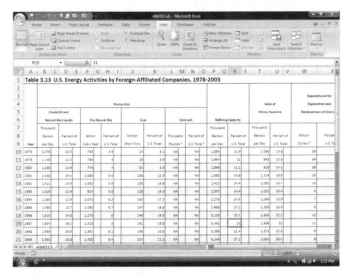

Figure 14.1
Determining the view you are working in.

Different Workbook Views

There are five different views you can apply to your workbook:

■ *Normal*: Optimised for working with data by allowing you to see as many cells as possible, while still providing you with the tools around your document.

■ *Page Layout View*: Provides a WYSIWYG view of your data so you know how things are going to look on the printed page (as shown in Figure 14.2, including being able to see headers and footers).

■ *Page Break Preview*: Allows you to easily see the page breaks in your workbook (as shown in Figure 14.3), which is quite important when you are dealing with an excessive amount of data. You need to know where your breaks are located and, where possible, adjust them so that tables do not spill over to additional pages when printed.

■ *Custom Views*: Allows you to save a set of custom views.

■ *Full Screen*: Regardless of the view you are working in (Normal or Page Layout), this option will try to expand your working area to its maximum, as shown in Figure 14.4. This can be very helpful when working with larger tables.

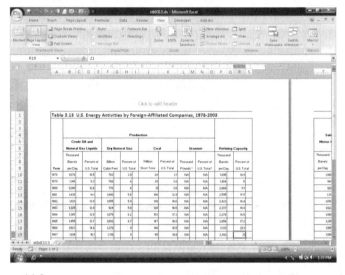

Figure 14.2
Page Layout View shows you WYSIWYG.

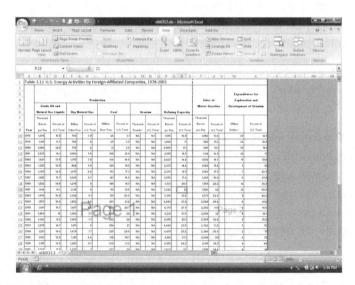

Figure 14.3
Page Break Preview lets you set your page breaks for printing.

Figure 14.4 (screenshot — Microsoft Excel - stb0313.xls)

Year	Crude Oil and Natural Gas Liquids – Thousand Barrels per Day	Percent of U.S. Total	Dry Natural Gas – Billion Cubic Feet	Percent of U.S. Total	Coal – Million Short Tons	Percent of U.S. Total	Uranium – Thousand Pounds	Percent of U.S. Total	Refining Capacity – Thousand Barrels per Day	Percent of U.S. Total	Sales of Motor Gasoline – Thousand Barrels per Day	Percent of U.S. Total	Expenditures for Exploration and Development of Uranium – Million Dollars	Percent of U.S. Total
1978	1,076	10.5	783	3.3	24	3.1	NA	NA	1,395	10.9	1,066	13.6	39	
1979	1,145	11.3	706	4	29	3.8	NA	NA	1,984	11	948	13.5	34	
1980	1,280	12.6	776	4	31	3.8	NA	NA	2,066	11.1	936	14.1	38	
1981	1,438	14.1	1,080	5.6	106	12.9	NA	NA	2,595	14.5	1,114	16.9	25	
1982	1,421	13.9	1,055	5.9	136	16.6	NA	NA	2,423	14.4	1,092	16.7	15	
1983	1,325	12.9	924	5.8	125	16.5	NA	NA	2,337	14.4	1,022	15.4	5	
1984	1,365	12.9	1,075	6.2	153	17.3	NA	NA	2,276	14.5	1,066	15.9	7	
1985	1,455	13.7	1,093	6.7	147	16.8	NA	NA	2,654	17.2	1,285	18.8	6	
1986	1,523	14.8	1,276	8	146	16.5	NA	NA	3,128	20.1	1,565	22.2	12	
1987	1,614	16.1	1,318	3	181	19.8	NA	NA	5,342	21	1,536	22	12	
1988	1,659	16.9	1,392	8.1	195	20.6	NA	NA	3,956	21.4	1,673	22.8	9	
1989	1,563	16.8	1,452	8.4	207	21.2	NA	NA	4,243	27.2	2,084	28.4	6	
1990	1,481	16.5	1,457	8.2	254	24.7	NA	NA	4,379	27.9	2,282	31.5	3	
1991	1,469	16	1,360	7.7	233	24	NA	NA	4,312	27.5	2,299	32	4	
1992	1,392	15.5	1,368	7.7	259	26	NA	NA	4,256	28.1	2,369	32.6	6	
1993	1,299	14.7	1,451	8	254	27	NA	NA	4,440	29.5	2,362	31.6	9	
1994	1,261	14.6	1,439	7.7	295	28.6	NA	NA	4,479	29.2	2,346	30.9	2	
1995	1,103	12.8	1,191	6.4	316	30.7	NA	NA	4,184	27.1	2,204	29	2	
1996	1,105	12.8	1,265	6.7	332	31.2	NA	NA	4,050	26.2	2,145	26.5	4	

Table 3.13 U.S. Energy Activities by Foreign-Affiliated Companies, 1978-2003

Figure 14.4
Full Screen gives you more real estate to work with.

Jargon buster

WYSIWYG (pronounced "wiz-ee-wig") is an acronym for "what you see is what you get". This type of view allows you to see how the results of your formatting and so forth will appear in the final document, or in some cases published web page.

14

Important

There are other configuration options you need to be aware of before printing. These are found on the Page Layout ribbon and include Margins, Orientation, Size and so forth. These options deal with the printing aspect of Excel 2007 which we will cover in Chapter 18.

Timesaver tip

To quickly switch between views, remember to use the status bar options ▦▣▦ . These options show three different views: Normal, Page Layout and Page Break Preview.

→ Zoom Controls

Zooming closer or further away from your data is easy in Excel 2007. You can use the options found under the View ribbon, Zoom grouping, or you can use the zoom slider found on the status bar.

To change the zoom level of a document, perform the following:

1 From the View ribbon, under the Zoom grouping, select the Zoom button for the Zoom dialogue shown in Figure 14.5.

2 You'll notice various percentages that are available for you to choose. If none of these suits your needs you can also select **Fit Selection** if you have a portion of your worksheet selected for Excel to zoom to, or you can establish a Custom setting. Note: The Custom setting allows you to choose a percentage between 10% and 400%.

3 Make your selection and choose OK.

Timesaver tip

If you want to quickly zoom from 10% to 400% you can use the Zoom Slider located on the status bar. You can use the slider itself by dragging it to the right and left for quick zooming, or you can use the plus (+) or minus (–) signs to zoom in smaller increments.

Another way to zoom quickly if you have a scroll mouse is to hold down your Ctrl button and use the scroll up and down button to zoom.

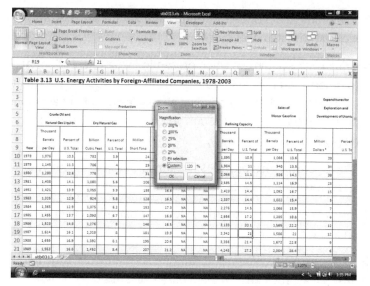

Figure 14.5
The Zoom dialogue.

Additional Zoom Features

Once you have zoomed in or out of a document you may want to quickly return to normal 100%. You can do this several ways. You can use the Zoom Slider to go back to 100%, you can use the Zoom dialogue box and choose 100%, or, right from the View ribbon, the Zoom grouping, you can select the 100% button.

You can zoom directly to a selection by choosing your cells and then using the **Zoom to Selection** option from the View ribbon under the Zoom grouping.

→ Show/Hide Options

On your View ribbon, under the Show/Hide grouping, are five checkboxes that can help you to configure your view to your liking. They include the following:

- *Ruler*: The ruler appears in Page Layout View and you can turn it off/on with this checkbox.

- *Gridlines*: Sometimes, when presenting your Excel information to others, you may want to turn these off. If you have formatted your tables and data properly it should leave behind a crisp presentation. Normally though you want your gridlines on to help you work more easily.

- *Message Bar*: This provides security alerts in the portion of space below the ribbon. You can turn it off/on if you like.

- *Formula Bar*: You can turn the formula bar off/on with this checkbox.

- *Headings*: Your column and row headings are controlled through this option. You can turn them off/on with this checkbox.

→ Window Options

Many novice Excel users are unaware of some of the configuration options that you can perform with your Excel view. For example, you have column and row headings that identify the important labels for your data. In a large table, as you scroll through, it would be helpful to have these headings travelling with you to remind you of what data you are looking at. This is called freezing your column or row heading so that it is visible, regardless of where you are in your worksheet.

Freeze Your Headings

To freeze your headings, perform the following:

1 From the View ribbon, under the Window grouping, select the Freeze Panes down arrow for a list of your options, as shown in Figure 14.6.

2 There are three options to choose from. They are:

■ *Freeze Panes:* To use this option you have to place your cursor at the proper intersection between the row and the column you want to freeze.

■ *Freeze Top Row*: Makes it easier to work with a larger table, because as you scroll from the top of your table down to the bottom, you are still able to see column headings.

■ *Freeze First Column*: Makes it easier to work with a larger table, because as you scroll from the left side to the right of your table you are still able to see your row headings.

3 Make your selection and notice how you can now manoeuvre through your worksheet but still have your headings following you, as shown in Figure 14.7.

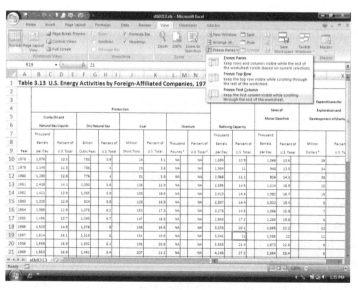

Figure 14.6
Your Freeze Panes options.

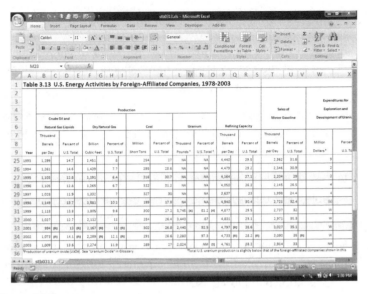

Figure 14.7

This shows a large table that you are scrolling down through with frozen column headings. Note, the cell background formatting was added in to make the distinction clearer.

Splitting the Worksheet Window

Sometimes you want to compare data from one part of your worksheet with data in another part of your worksheet. You can split your data into two panes (either horizontally or vertically) by using a split bar. You can establish two split bars that allow you to actually have four panes when you are done, as shown in Figure 14.8.

With split panes, the changes you make in one pane are reflected in the other. You are not seeing separate documents, just separate views of the same data. You can also drag cells and ranges between these panes.

To split a window, perform the following:

1 Place your cursor in the cell below or to the right of where you want the split to occur.

2 Go to the View ribbon, under the Window grouping, and select the Split button.

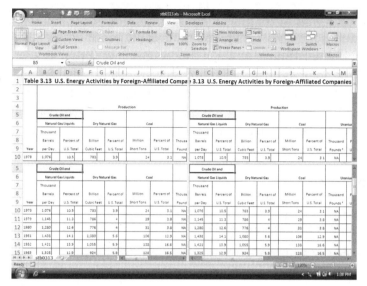

Figure 14.8
Splitting up your worksheet window.

3 If you want only one of the split bars, double-click the one you do not want and you can have the other one remain.

4 You can now use one pane or the other to display your data so that you can see it side by side.

Timesaver tip

Another way to split your document view quickly is by using the split boxes located at the intersection of your scroll bars and at the top of your horizontal bar. These little boxes, when selected, can be dragged into your worksheet to split the window.

Additional Window Options

You may have noticed a lot of other options on your View ribbon, under the Window grouping. They include the following configuration options:

- *New Window*: Will open a new window of the document you are working in. It will append the name of the document with a :(number). In other words, if the document was originally entitled workbook.xls, you will see two versions of this document: workbook.xls:1 and workbook.xls:2. Keep in mind that these are still the same workbook, so changing data in one will change it in the other. If you want to save one of these as a different document you can do that to protect your original data.

- *Arrange All*: Will allow you to choose how you want your workbooks to be organised. You can see all workbooks in a tiled, horizontal, vertical, etc. arrangement.

- *Hide*: Will hide the current window you are in.

- *Unhide*: Will unhide the windows you have hidden.

- *View Side by Side*: Allows you to view two different worksheets side by side.

- *Synchronous Scrolling*: Lets you scroll on one worksheet but it scrolls on the other one too. Benefits you only if you are working side by side.

- *Reset Window Position*: If you have changed the amount of space one window takes up in comparison with another when using the side by side feature, this will reset the positions so that both windows take up equal space.

- *Save Workspace*: Allows you to save the current configuration of your workspace so that you can restore it later. When you select this button you are asked to provide a name for your saved workspace and the data will be saved as an *.xlw file.

- *Switch Windows*: When you have multiple Excel workbooks open, this option will allow you to switch to another workbook that you already have open.

Timesaver tip

You can switch between workbooks using the standard Alt+Tab quick keys to tab through your open documents until you find the right one. If you are using Windows Vista you can use the 3D-flip method of the Windows Key+Tab to see a 3D visualisation of your windows open.

14

15

Insert Illustrations and SmartArt

In this lesson you will learn how to take your Excel spreadsheet to the next level by adding eye-catching illustrations and SmartArt. These may illustrate a point in your worksheet, or they may visually demonstrate your data.

Although this will not happen often, at times you may want to insert illustrations (pictures, clip art, shapes) into your worksheets. These may enhance your presentation if you choose to present information through Excel, as opposed to a Word document or a PowerPoint presentation.

To insert a picture, clip art or a shape you go to the Insert ribbon, under the Illustrations grouping. Let's consider each type of illustration and how you can use these in your Excel workbooks.

Insert Pictures

You may have a document that you want to enhance visually for a variety of reasons. For example, Figure 15.1 shows an invoice that includes an added logo.

Figure 15.1
Use mild inclusions of graphics to enhance your documents.

To insert a graphic (picture, photo, etc.), perform the following:

1 On the worksheet in which you wish to insert the graphic, place your cursor in the cell near where you want the graphic to appear.

2 On the Insert ribbon, under the Illustrations grouping, select the Picture button.

3 The Insert Picture dialogue will appear and you can locate your picture by searching automatically or manually through your files and folders. Notice in the dialogue (shown in Figure 15.2) that you can see a preview of your picture to ensure it is the correct one. Once you locate your picture, select the Insert button.

Figure 15.2
Locate and include your picture in your worksheet.

Once your picture is included, it will be possible for you to perform a variety of formatting on the picture through the Format contextual ribbon. We will discuss formatting shortly.

Insert Clip Art

Clip art is reusable drawings, photos, sound clips and movies that Microsoft provides to you in an easy-to-search and insert gallery. To insert clip art into your worksheet, perform the following:

1 On the worksheet in which you wish to insert the clip art, place your cursor in the cell near where you want the graphic to appear.

2 On the Insert ribbon, under the Illustrations grouping, select the Clip Art button.

3 The Clip Art task pane appears. In the **Search for** window you can type the image you are looking for (in the example in Figure 15.3 we are searching for a diamond image).

4 Under the **Search in** options you can narrow down where your clip art searches. Usually, it's best to leave "Everywhere" selected so you get the widest level of return from your search.

5 Under the **Results should be** options you can determine the type of media files to search for. For example, if you aren't interested in searching for movies or sounds, you can de-select those options.

6 As you scan the gallery for your clip art, if you want to choose one you like, just select it and it will appear in your worksheet, near where your cursor was last positioned.

With your clip art image added into your document, you can perform additional formatting through the Format contextual ribbon, just like when you insert a picture. We will discuss this ribbon shortly.

Insert Shapes

There are so many options you can pursue in using shapes. You can add everything from a square to a lightning bolt. In addition to adding these shapes for effect, you can insert text into the shapes. Consider the example in Figure 15.4. Here we use arrow shapes and callout banners to make points stand out in the Excel worksheet.

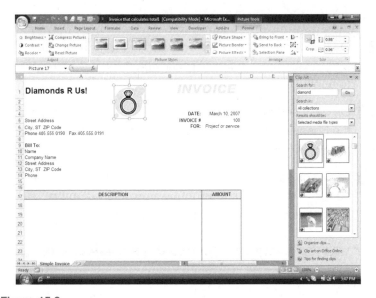

Figure 15.3
Working with clip art.

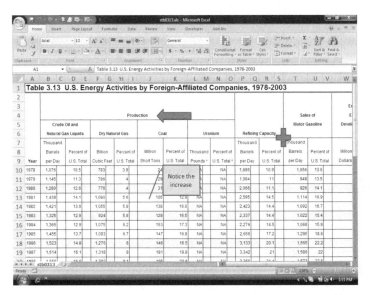

Figure 15.4
Using shapes to make points stand out.

To insert a shape, perform the following:

1 On the worksheet in which you wish to insert the shape, place your cursor in the cell near where you want the shape to appear.

2 On the Insert ribbon, under the Illustrations grouping, select the Shapes button. This will present all your shape options (shown in Figure 15.5).

3 Once you select your shape you will be able to use your cursor to drag your shape onto your worksheet in the location you choose to whatever size you like.

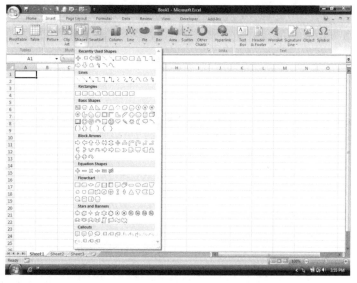

Figure 15.5
An array of shapes to choose from.

Once your shape is added to the worksheet you can perform additional formatting using the Format contextual ribbon.

→ Formatting Your Pictures, Clip Art and Shapes

The Format contextual ribbon that appears when you insert a picture, clip art or shape offers you formatting options that relate to the specific image you have chosen to include. For example, the Format ribbon for your picture and clip art is slightly different from the one for your shapes because they each have different configuration options. While you might change the fill colour of a shape, this isn't possible with a picture.

Picture and Clip Art Formatting Options

If you select your picture or clip art, you will be able to select the Format ribbon. There are four groupings available to you for formatting your image, as follows:

- *Adjust*: Allows you to alter the brightness and contrast. In addition, you can Recolour the picture using a gallery of options, shown in Figure 15.6. You also have the option to compress the image so that your document size stays low. You can change the picture for a different one and reset the picture to its original look (if you have changed some of the aspects of the picture).

- *Picture Styles*: Provides you with a gallery of styles, shown in Figure 15.7, that offer predesigned effects for your picture. If you want to apply your own effects, you can use the options Picture Shape, Picture Border and Picture Effects to adjust the image into the one you prefer. Note: For granular control over your picture, select the handle in the bottom right-hand corner of the Picture Styles grouping.

- *Arrange*: Especially with multiple images on one screen, there are times when you need to have one resting behind the other (Send to Back) or pull one closer to the viewer (Bring to Front). In addition, you may want to flip the image around, align the image better with other images, or group images together. All of this can be performed with the Arrange grouping tools.

15

■ *Size*: These options allow you to crop the image, or alter the height and width of the image. However, if you select the handle in the bottom right-hand corner of the grouping you will notice more tools in resizing your images, including the ability to rotate your image.

Timesaver tip

When you select your images you will notice a variety of points will surround the image. One, at the top, is a green circle. If you select this point and hold your mouse button down, you can rotate your image. There are also corner points (circles) located at the four corners of your image which you can use to resize your images, and there are middle points (squares) you can use to skew your images.

Figure 15.6
The Recolor gallery.

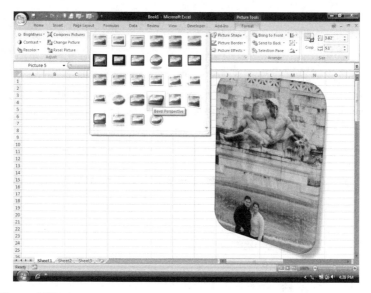

Figure 15.7
Using the Picture Styles gallery.

Shape Formatting Options

Because shapes are a different type of image from pictures or clip art, they come with their own formatting options. Note: The Arrange and Size options are the same between the two with the exception of the cropping tools, because a shape doesn't need to be cropped. These options include the following:

■ *Insert Shapes*: Gives you an opportunity to add more shapes to the worksheet. You can also select the Edit Shape button to give you greater control over your shape, allowing you to edit the points that make up the shape itself.

■ *Shape Styles*: You can choose from the Shape Styles gallery, shown in Figure 15.8, from a variety of predesigned effects. Or you can use the Shape Fill, Shape Outline and Shape Effects options to design your own effect.

■ *WordArt Styles*: If you have text within your shapes you can alter the colour of that text, the fill effect and more. Or you can quickly apply a word art style from the WordArt Styles gallery, shown in Figure 15.9.

15

Important

You can insert a text box, which is a free floating box that allows you to include text that you can move around your worksheet to highlight points, using the Insert ribbon, under the Text grouping. However, a text box is also a shape feature. You can add one from the Shapes button.

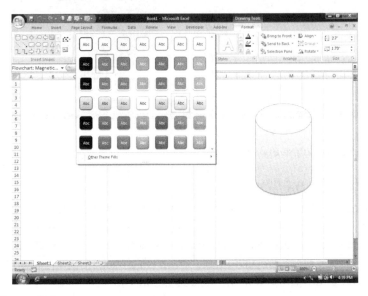

Figure 15.8
The Shape Styles gallery.

→ Adding SmartArt into Your Worksheets

SmartArt is used to create diagrams, organisational charts, flow charts and so forth. SmartArt can really enhance your presentations (especially in a Word document or PowerPoint presentation), allowing you to create eye-catching images that you can format with any number of possibilities. An example of SmartArt within a spreadsheet can be seen in Figure 15.10.

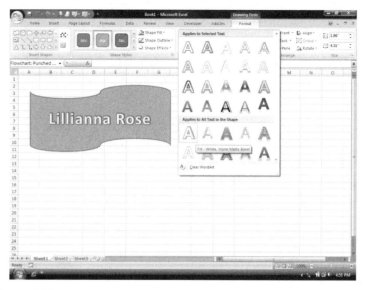

Figure 15.9
The WordArt Styles gallery.

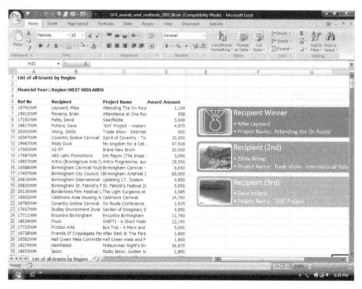

Figure 15.10
SmartArt makes an impact.

To insert and configure SmartArt in your worksheet, perform the following:

1 On the worksheet in which you wish to insert the SmartArt, place your cursor in the cell near where you want the image to appear.

2 On the Insert ribbon, under the Illustrations grouping, select the SmartArt button. This will present you with the **Choose a SmartArt Graphic** dialogue box, shown in Figure 15.11.

3 You can choose from seven different layouts, with a host of options within those layouts. Although confusing at times, notice the helpful description (and image preview) on the right side of the dialogue box. After making your selection, hit OK.

4 Once your SmartArt is in your worksheet you can add text by simply selecting any of the images you want and working within the drawing canvas, shown in Figure 15.12.

Jargon buster

Drawing canvas acts as a frame that forms a boundary between your SmartArt drawing shapes and holds them together in one location. It is a nice way to keep shapes that have a similar purpose in one location.

Also note in Figure 15.12 the Design contextual ribbon that appears with SmartArt (as a secondary contextual ribbon along with the Format ribbon). These design options allow you to determine the colouring scheme of your shapes, let you alter the shape you have chosen or even select a different style type for the SmartArt object.

Figure 15.11
Creating a SmartArt graphic.

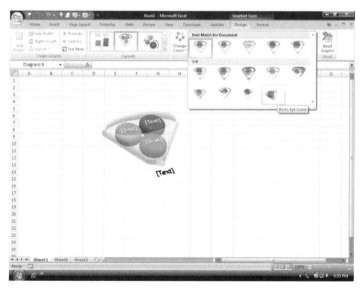

Figure 15.12
Working within the drawing canvas.

16

Basic Charting

In this lesson you will learn the basics of creating charts. You will learn how to create a simple column chart and a pie chart.

→ Excel Chart Building

Excel does more than provide you with a way of manipulating and viewing data, more than advanced functions to build formulas... Excel supplies a method of creating graphical representations of that data, essentially converting numeric input into a visual structure. Charts make your data more understandable and enhance the visual aspect of your presentations.

Understanding Chart Types

There are many different chart types. You can use lines to plot your data visually, bar charts, columns, pie charts and more (selected ones shown in Figure 16.1). Some data can be stacked on top of each other, or represented side by side as a means of comparison, in lines to show a trend, 2D or 3D... almost limitless ideas exist.

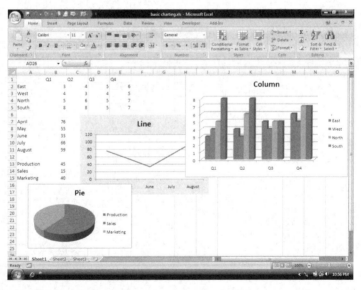

Figure 16.1
Some of the charting options on a single worksheet.

Important

By default, all new charts are created as embedded objects in the current sheet you are working in. You can move your chart to a different sheet, or actually move the chart to its own sheet (called a chart sheet). To do this, once the chart is created, you go to the Design contextual ribbon, select the Move Chart button and then specify a different location (either as a new chart sheet, or an object in another worksheet).

Here are the chart types that Excel offers (keep in mind that some of these are somewhat complicated to implement without having advanced knowledge of numerical charting):

■ *Column*: Is used to show comparisons between two or more series of data. This type of chart is best chosen when you want to show comparisons of only a few series (1–10 or so) that demonstrate a trend over a period of time.

■ *Line*: Also used to display a trend for one or more series of data. Uses a line that is easily visible to represent growth or decline.

■ *Pie*: Shows the relationship of each piece of data to a whole. Pie charts have only one series of data to work from and are simple to create, but are very powerful at making their point in a presentation.

■ *Bar*: Similar to a column chart, only turned on its side. Bar charts are better used (as opposed to column charts) when you want to show the results with a "winner" highlighted. The bar presentation looks like the winner crossing the finish line in the mind of the viewer.

■ *Area*: Adds together the values of a data series to represent a cumulative change and is good for highlighting changes over periods of time.

■ *X Y (Scatter)*: Used mostly for scientific purposes, this type of chart doesn't worry about time, but instead plots correlations between different series of values.

16

- *Stock*: Stocks often have an opening price, a closing, a high and a low. This type of chart allows you to show ups and downs in a stock over the course of time based upon volume, price and time.

- *Surface*: Lets you add a topographic layer over a column or area chart, showing a 3D surface.

- *Doughnut*: Similar to a pie chart but with more than one data series, each ring representing a series. You use a doughnut chart when you want to compare pie chart data series.

- *Bubble*: Similar to scatter charts, only with a third data series that allows you to see more than a dot to represent the connection between the X and Y values; the third series determines the size of the bubbles.

- *Radar*: Actually extends its axis from the centre of the chart and usually represents a rating along different performance areas. Using a radar chart should show you where you are performing well and where you are lacking, especially in relation to a competitor's radar ratings.

Chart Terminology

To create a chart may be simple in Excel 2007, but to understand how to create a chart and then format it afterwards you need to understand some of the terminology that goes along with charting data. Consider Figure 16.2 and we will discuss the various terms in the chart.

- *Axis*: This is one side of a chart. You have the horizontal axis (called the x-axis) and the vertical axis (called the y-axis). The horizontal axis includes the data series and categories for the chart. The vertical axis includes the values. You can have multiple x and y axes in a chart and some charts you might even have a z-axis to represent another dimension to your chart.

- *Legend*: Defines what each series is in your chart. In the column chart we see the legend represents the different data series for each column.

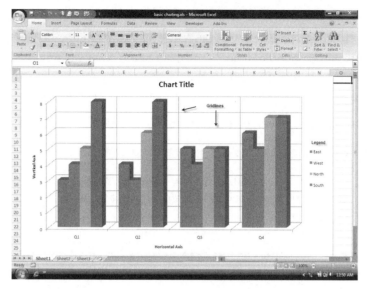

Figure 16.2
Charting terminology.

- *Gridlines*: Helpful in pinpointing a little better the exact value of a point because they generally emanate from the y-axis to help you match up your data series with the numerical labels on the axis. You can turn them on/off for your y and x axis.

- *Data Series*: Although not specifically labelled in the chart, your data series is the representation of your data in the chart. In this case there are four different data series being represented, one for East, West, North and South.

→ Create a Simple Chart   16

In this next section we will walk through two simple scenarios, one for creating a column chart (like the one seen in the figure above) and one for creating a pie chart. We will make some formatting changes, but we will leave the major chart formatting for Chapter 17. Let's proceed with the column chart.

Create a Column Chart

You will need to start with a table that includes a comparison of data over a period of time. In the case of the chart we are creating we will have two different companies (Company A and Company B) over a January to December comparison for products sold.

To create the column chart, perform the following:

1 Select the table, including row and column headings.

2 On the Insert ribbon, under the Charts grouping, select the Column button. Notice the many different types of column charts you have available in Figure 16.3.

Figure 16.3
Creating a column chart gives you many different options.

3 You can decide which type of chart you would like. In this example we will choose a simple 2D clustered column chart.

4 Immediately after you select your chart type the chart will be created for you and placed within your worksheet (as shown in Figure 16.4).

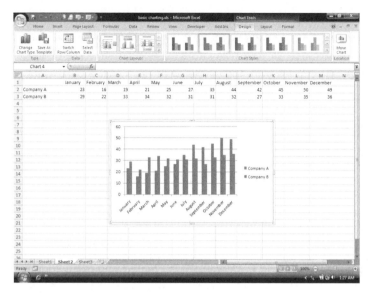

Figure 16.4
Your basic two-dimensional column chart.

You might notice that three contextual ribbons have appeared: Design, Layout and Format. Each of these offers a plethora of tools to work with to alter the appearance of your chart. We will discuss these further in the next chapter, but you are welcome to begin testing them out now. Many of them are quite easy to understand. If you don't like the results, you can also select the Undo button.

Timesaver tip

If you want to quickly create a column chart (the default chart type) you can select the data for the chart and press F11. This will create your chart and place it in its own sheet for editing.

16

Create a Pie Chart

A pie chart involves a simple list of data that Excel converts into a graphic representation that shows how that data fits into the "whole" of a pie. For example, let's say you spend a certain amount of money on your bills each month (for example $2,000). Logically, it's not going to be an even 2,000 and it doesn't have to be. If you place all your bills into a list and create a pie chart, Excel determines from the whole what each of the parts will be.

To create the pie chart, perform the following:

1 Select the list you've created, including labels with each bill.

2 On the Insert ribbon, under the Charts grouping, select the Pie button. There is a variety of pie chart types to choose from, including two- and three-dimensional.

3 You can choose whichever one you like best. In this example we have chosen a simple 2D pie chart, as shown in Figure 16.5.

4 Once your chart is selected, it is created and ready for editing.

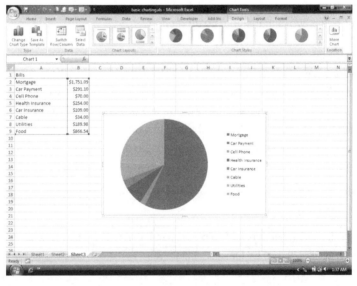

Figure 16.5
Your basic two-dimensional pie chart.

→ Making Some Design Changes

The chart that Excel creates is a standard, no-frills representation of the data. But you have a ton of options available to add some style to your charts.

For example, you can use the Design ribbon to choose a new layout and style for your chart. To change the style or layout, perform the following:

1 Select the chart you have created.

2 Go to the Design contextual ribbon and select the Chart Styles gallery down arrow.

3 You are presented with a large number of different styles, as shown in Figure 16.6. Select a new style to apply to your chart.

4 If you want to change the layout of your chart, you can select the Chart Layouts gallery down arrow. Again, you are presented with options that will change where the legend is, how the columns are spaced, whether gridlines are on or off, and so forth, as shown in Figure 16.7.

5 You can try a variety of styles and layouts and none of these options will hurt your chart in any way. You can always undo what you've selected.

Important

Each chart type is different and so the design options are going to be different as well. The pie chart layout, for example, offers you layouts that are more appropriate to pie charts.

If you note the colours offered by the styles, these colours are chosen because they are connected with the current theme. You can change the theme of your Excel workbook by going to the Page Layout ribbon and, under Themes, selecting a new theme. Then the colours in your Chart Styles will automatically update.

16

Figure 16.6
The Chart Styles gallery has a lot to offer for a quick restylising of
your chart.

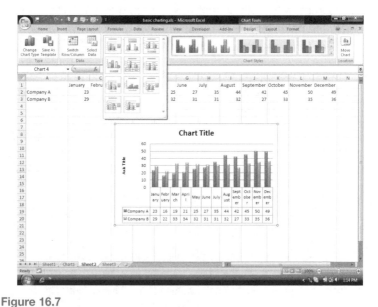

Figure 16.7
The Chart Layouts gallery can quickly help you reposition and redesign
the look of your chart.

Changing the Type of Data

The Design ribbon has a few options in the top left corner that may help you to adjust your chart to your needs. For example, if you decide you want to go with a 3D version of the chart you've chosen, or change the design from a column chart to a bar chart, you can look under the Type grouping for the Change Chart Type options, which will take you back to the Change Chart Type gallery that presents all your charting options.

You can save the chart as a template for future use by using the Save As Template option and then saving the template as a *.crtx file. Then, when you go to create a chart in the future, you can select from the templates gallery the chart you have saved and all the formatting you've done will be brought back and applied to your new chart.

If you want to see what would happen if you changed the default way your data is viewed by switching the row/column view of the data, then look under the Data grouping and select the Switch Row/Column option.

If you have to add more data to your chart, you can add it to your table and then, rather than recreating your entire chart, you can use Select Data (under the Data grouping) and alter the selection options. The Select Data Source dialogue will appear, as shown in Figure 16.8.

From within the dialogue you can switch the row/column view. You can also change the legend to display one company above another regardless of how it is in the table itself. Some companies may prefer to have their name first in the list above that of their competitors.

16

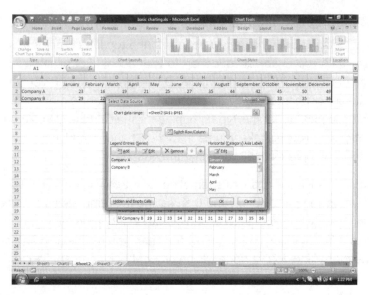

Figure 16.8
Use the Select Data Source dialogue to alter the charts data series.

17

Advanced Chart Formatting

In this lesson you will take your charting knowledge to the next level with advanced features of charting, including changing labels on the axis of your chart, adding a legend, manipulating colours and backgrounds to your charts, and making a combination chart (to really catch their attention)!

→ Changing Labels

Having a chart that looks nice is important, but having one that represents your data properly is the primary goal. To really make that data clear to your audience you may want to label the chart itself, make sure your x and y axes have labels to clearly show the timeframe, or the amount of money being spent, or place data labels on your data series directly. Labelling options can be found on the Layout contextual ribbon.

Adding a Chart Title

To add a chart title to your chart, perform the following:

1 Select the chart you have created.

2 Go to the Layout contextual ribbon and from the Labels grouping, select the Chart Title option. You will be presented with two different types of labels, shown in Figure 17.1.

■ *Centred Overlay Title*: Keeps your chart the same size and places the title over the chart at the top.

■ *Above Chart*: Reduces the size of your chart in order to place the title above.

3 Titles are placed in 18pt Cambria font, but you can change this using the mini-toolbar or the Font options from the Home ribbon. You can also go to the Format contextual ribbon and change the font into WordArt.

4 When you add in a title it appears as Chart Title. You have to select the title and add your own, as shown in Figure 17.2. Notice that you can also move the title around to another location if you prefer.

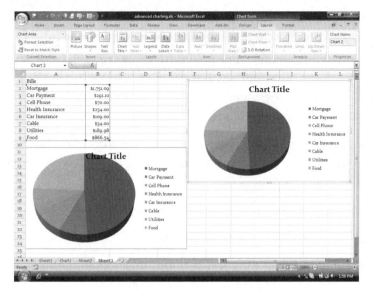

Figure 17.1
Chart title labelling options.

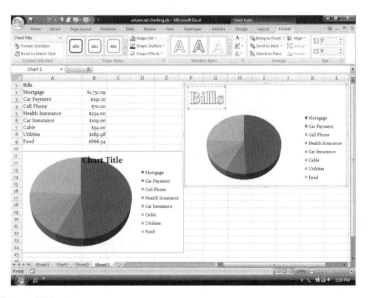

Figure 17.2
Changing your chart title's properties.

Adding Labels to Your Axes

When looking at a chart with axes, you may want to add labels to make the chart more understandable. For example, if you look at the y-axis and see numbers incrementing from 1–10, it would be very helpful to know whether those numbers represent millions or billions of dollars.

You can add the label to your vertical or horizontal axis. For your vertical axis you can choose to have the label displayed vertically, horizontally or rotated.

To add labels to your axis, perform the following:

1 Select the chart you have created.

2 Go to the Layout contextual ribbon and from the Labels grouping, select the Axis Titles options.

3 From the Primary Horizontal Axis Title, select the Title Below Axis option. (Notice you have only one type of horizontal axis option.)

4 From the Primary Vertical Axis Title, you have various options:

■ *Rotated Title*: Rotates the text sideways so that it aligns with the y-axis (as shown in Figure 17.3).

■ *Vertical Title*: Places the text in an up-and-down view without rotating the characters.

■ *Horizontal Title*: Places the text in a standard left-to-right format.

5 Once you have the axis labels in place you can edit these just like you edited your title by selecting the text and typing the real labels and using the formatting options to alter the font.

Figure 17.3
Adding horizontal and vertical axis labels. The y-axis label is the rotated title option.

Timesaver tip

To quickly add chart titles and axis labels to a chart you can use the Chart Layouts gallery on the Design ribbon. Select a layout that will already include the labels you need. Then you simply have to edit those labels according to your preference.

Changing Your Legend

A legend will identify the colour on your chart with the data marker. You don't absolutely need a legend (you could choose to label each set of data individually using other means). However, you can also determine the locations and layout for your legend by using the Legend options found under the Labels grouping on the Layout ribbon, as shown in Figure 17.4.

17

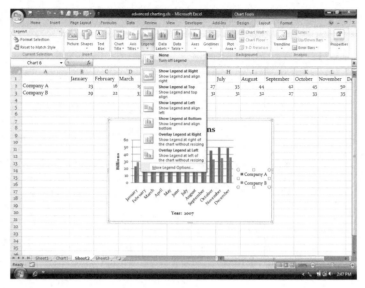

Figure 17.4
Legend labelling options.

Legends, by default in Excel 2007, have a transparent fill. If you want, you can change this by using the Shapes tools on the Format ribbon.

Adding Data Labels

Data Labels (also located on the Layout ribbon under the Labels grouping) allow you to add exact values of the data right into the chart. You can use these labels in a pie chart to show the value of each pie slice, or you can use them to show percentages. In Figure 17.5 you see that you have the ability to add the labels into the middle of the bars (or in a pie chart, into the middle of the slice) or to other locations around and on top of the data bar.

Include the Data Table

Certain charts (column, bar, line, area and stock charts) allow you the extra option under the Labels grouping of the Layout ribbon to include the data table directly underneath the chart, as shown in Figure 17.6. The benefit here is that your audience will be able to see the visual representation combined with the actual data.

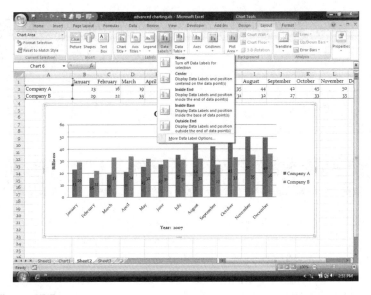

Figure 17.5
Adding data labels.

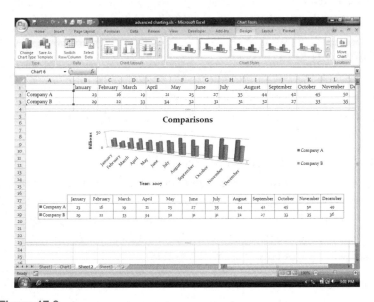

Figure 17.6
Include the data table to a chart to show your literal data with its
graphical representation.

Important

Showing the data table is beneficial only if you have a small amount of data to show. If your charts are made up of a large amount of data, it would be better to share the actual figures on a separate page.

→ Changing Colours and Backgrounds

In Chapter 16 we discussed the way you can quickly alter the colour and style of a chart by using the Chart Styles gallery. You can also alter the colours presented within that gallery by changing the Theme for your workbook. However, you may want to make some personal modifications to the way your chart looks. You can pick your own colours and the style of your data series. You can alter the background of your entire chart to display a picture if you like. Let's explore how this is done.

Changing Fills

To change the colour and effects for a data series requires some accurate mouse clicking on your part. To select, for example, one piece of a pie chart, you first select the pie itself and all the points of the pie will appear, as shown in Figure 17.7.

With all the points selected you can right-click the pie chart and choose "Format Data Series" and you will be presented with only a few formatting options. You can rotate the angle of that first slice to turn it just right for your audience to see. And you can determine the amount of "pie explosion" which will actually separate the pie pieces from each other.

Click the pie a second time, directly on the data piece you like. (Keep in mind that this same approach is used for other charts, the first click selects the entire chart, the second will select the exact series. In a column chart you might click a third time to

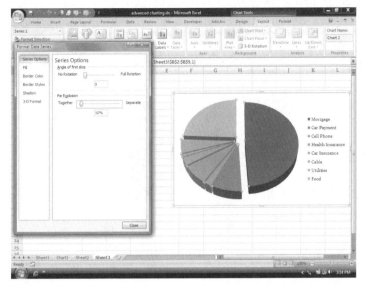

Figure 17.7
Selecting all the pie slices allows you to right-click and format the
data series.

select a specific bar in a series.) Notice in Figure 17.8 that only
one piece of the pie is selected. If you right-click that piece and
select Format Data Point, you can then change the fill, border,
styles and so forth for just that data point.

Changing the Chart Background

Sometimes you might want your chart background to stand out to
make the point of the chart a little more powerful. To do this you
can use standard fill effects with colours, or colour patterns, or
you can use one of the default background textures that come
with the Office suite. These backgrounds show different wood
effects and so forth. Or you can use pictures of your choosing to
fill in the background. See Figure 17.9.

17

To do this, select within the white space of your chart, right-click
and choose **Format Chart Area**. Note: If you see other options
such as **Format Plot Area**, you are too close to the chart itself,
move your cursor more into the white space.

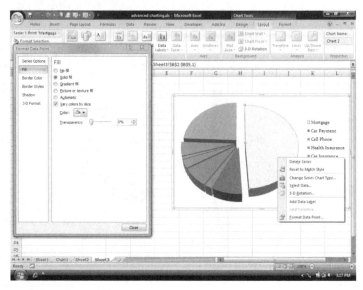

Figure 17.8
Changing the formatting of a specific data point in your chart.

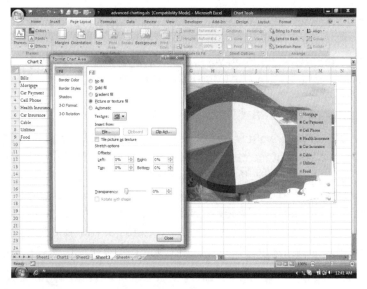

Figure 17.9
Change the background fill of your chart.

→ Make a Combination Chart

Sometimes you may want to make a chart that includes two different chart types. For example, you may want to make a stock market chart that shows more than the ticker price through the day but includes a column chart of the volume traded (this is a line-column chart type). These types of charts are called "combination charts".

Without going too far beyond the scope of this book, we are confident you have the ability to create one of these with Excel 2007.

One very interesting type of combination chart is called the pie-of-bar chart type. Sometimes you may have so many little pieces to a pie that it becomes unreadable and then you haven't helped your presentation but hurt it because of the complicated view.

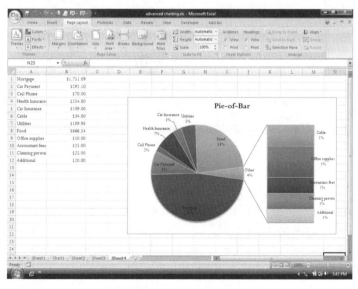

Figure 17.10
A pie-of-bar combination chart.

Consider Figure 17.10. This is a pie-of-bar chart. We created this chart by placing all our data in the table in the worksheet, as you can see. Then we selected this as an option from among our chart types. Initially, it didn't look right, because we had to alter the distinction between the first plot series that would go into the main pie chart and the second plot series that would go into the bar chart. To do this we right-clicked the pie and selected the Format Data Series option (shown in Figure 17.11).

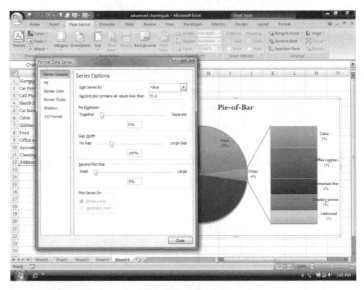

Figure 17.11
The Series Options of a pie-of-bar combination chart.

Under the Series Options, we chose to split the two series by value (choosing a value of $51), causing all data under a certain value to be moved to the second plot, the bar chart. We could have chosen percentage, position or a custom value.

You can alter the other options of the chart by working with the pie explosion, the gap width and the second plot size.

18

Printing Your Worksheets

In this lesson you will learn how to print your documents. Because spreadsheets can grow both vertically and horizontally, they may not print out the way a Word document does… but have no worries, you will learn how to print them out so they display the data in the way you need.

→ Manually Adjusting the Print Structure

Microsoft Word is completely structured around the printing of your pages, whereas Excel worksheets allow for you to grow your tables to whatever size you like, with no concern for these to be put onto paper. Eventually, though, you may want to print that data and you'll find that you need to be creative in getting your information to print properly if it is quite large. If you just print your worksheet, Excel will give no concern as to where that data should break properly so that it is represented well. You need to be personally involved in defining print areas to divide your worksheet into printable areas.

Jargon buster

Quick Print and **Print** dialogue: You'll learn shortly that you can use the Quick Print key to send your worksheet to the printer without answering any questions in dialogue boxes. The Print options present dialogue boxes for you to answer certain questions before printing. You'll find in Excel that it is often better to use the standard Print option that comes with a dialogue box because Excel printing requires a bit more hands-on configuration than Word.

Define Your Print Area

Excel, by default, assumes you want to print the entire worksheet (starting with A1 of your worksheet until the end of your data), but if this isn't the case you can alter the print area. To define your print area, perform the following:

1 Select the range you wish to print, regardless of the size of that range.

2 Go to your Page Layout ribbon, under the Page Setup grouping, and select the Print Area option. Then choose **Set Print Area**.

3 If you make an error and want to change the print area, select the option **Clear Print Area**.

Important

The default print concept in Excel when you use the Quick Print or Print dialogue options is for Excel to print all the data on your worksheet. When you define your print area, Excel will ignore areas you haven't selected. So, if you add more information to your worksheet and you do not redefine your print area, that new information (rows and columns) won't show up in your printed document. You must remember to reset your print area after you make adjustments to your data.

Using Print Preview

To check whether your print area is set right for printing you can use the Print Preview option, shown in Figure 18.1.

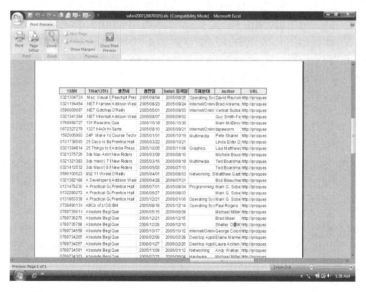

Figure 18.1
Using the Print Preview option to ensure your document will print properly.

To use Print Preview, perform the following:

1 From within the worksheet you are looking to print, select the Office Button.

2 Move your mouse over the print options and then select Print Preview from the printing options shown.

3 From within the Print Preview you can see your print options, your page setup, you can zoom in or out of your documents, view margins and move to other pages that will be printed.

Timesaver tip

If you find yourself using Print Preview often, you can add this option to the Quick Access Toolbar for quick selection.

Changing Your Print Area

When you establish a print area, this area may not be exactly what you were looking for. You can clear the print area and try again, or you might want to be creative in moving where certain areas break. Excel simply adds those breaks where you run out of room for it to print on the page.

To use manual page breaks you can place your cursor in the cell below and to the right of the last cell you want on the page and then, from the Page Layout ribbon, under the Page Setup grouping, you can select the Breaks button and then "Insert Page Break" option. You remove these manual page breaks from within the same options.

We noted the different views available in Excel in Chapter 14 and one of them is called the Page Break Preview, shown in Figure 18.2.

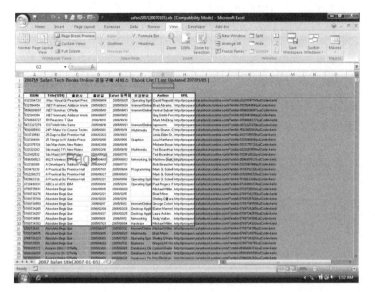

Figure 18.2
Getting your print area structured properly by using the Page Break
Preview view.

This view shows you exactly where Excel is breaking pages and
how your worksheet will print. You can make changes by
dragging the lines to better suit your needs. Ordinarily, you don't
want to try to force Excel to print too much. You might want to
determine where your pages would break better by shrinking the
size of the page area.

Portrait or Landscape?

When you establish a print area, you may notice that your table is
longer than the print area allows. Perhaps you don't want to print
the table with a portrait view in mind, but need to change your
spreadsheet on a landscape page. To do this, perform the following:

1 From within the worksheet, go to the Page Layout ribbon,
under the Page Setup grouping, and select the Orientation
option. Select **Landscape**.

2 Notice how this affects the spreadsheet we have been working
with in this chapter, in Figure 18.3, while in Page Break Preview.

18

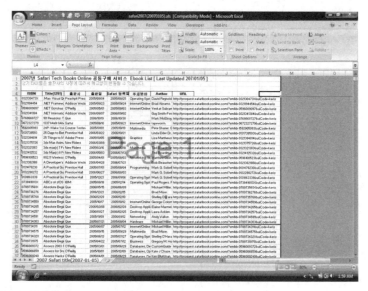

Figure 18.3
Sometimes with spreadsheets, Landscape is the better way to print.

→ Adjusting Page Setup Options

The Page Setup grouping under the Page Layout ribbon offers you many different options such as Margins, Paper Size and Print Titles. Most of these offer you a few selections and then a final option to go to the Page Setup dialogue box. Another way to get there is by selecting the handle in the lower right-hand corner of the grouping. This will lead you to a dialogue with four tabs that can help to set up your document for more controlled printing.

The Page Layout Tab

The first tab has some simple options, such as Orientation, where you can choose Portrait or Landscape (much like the button on the ribbon offers). But, as you can see from Figure 18.4, you have options to scale your document as well.

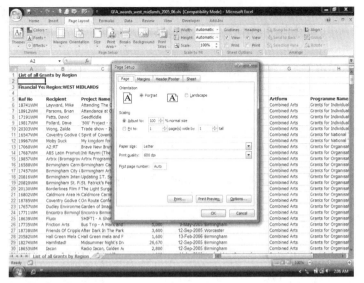

Figure 18.4
The Page Layout tab allows you to change the document's orientation, scaling and some print options.

Changing the scale will allow you to print more on your pages by scaling down (or up if you choose, but this will take up more space on pages) according to a percentage you establish. You may just have to work with this percentage setting until you feel your document will print on the pages you want without losing quality.

Timesaver tip

A quick way to perform scaling of your data is through the Scale To Fit grouping off the Page Layout ribbon. You can adjust the width, height and scale.

You can also choose the **Fit to** options to determine the pages wide by how many pages tall. If, for example, you establish 1 page wide by a blank number of pages tall, then Excel will make sure your spreadsheet goes only the width of one page but will print as long as needed.

18

You can also change the paper size, the print quality in dpi's (dots per inch) and the **First Page Number**.

The Margins Tab

You can select some simple margin changes from the Margins button off the Page Layout ribbon, under the Page Setup grouping. For more detailed margin settings you can use the Margins tab from the Page Setup dialogue, as shown in Figure 18.5.

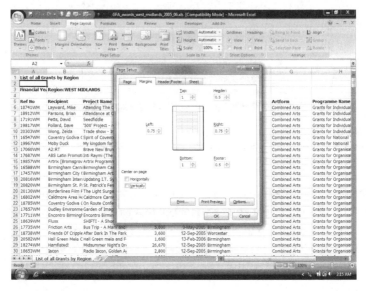

Figure 18.5
More detailed margin configurations can be achieved from the Margins tab, under the Page Setup dialogue.

The scrolling options to establish distance from the end of the page to the document print area are easy to understand. There are also two options under the **Center on page** heading. One is **Horizontally**, which will centre the table on the page from left to right. The other is **Vertically**, which will centre the table on the page from top to bottom.

The Header/Footer Tab

From the Header/Footer tab, shown in Figure 18.6, you can choose from preselected header/footer options by selecting the down arrows next to the header or footer details.

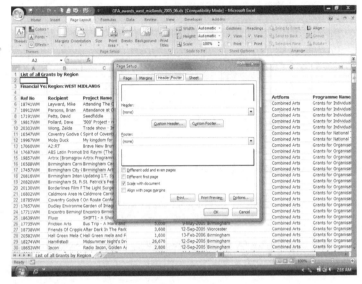

Figure 18.6
Adding a header or a footer to your document before printing.

You can configure your own header or footer by choosing the **Custom Header** and/or **Custom Footer** buttons. From here you add your own fields and formatting to the header/footer. You can also add a graphic (for example, a company logo), as you can see in Figure 18.7.

The Sheet Tab

The Sheet tab, shown in Figure 18.8, contains many different options that you can use to configure the way you want your worksheet printed.

18

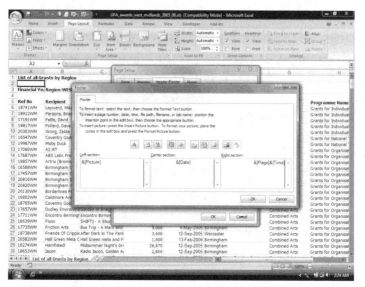

Figure 18.7
Creating your own customised headers and footers.

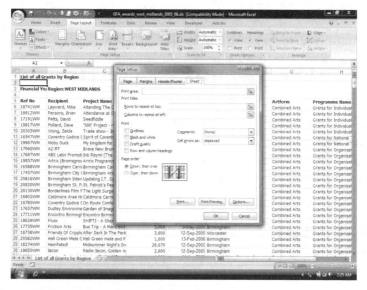

Figure 18.8
Configuring options on the Sheet tab.

Table 18.1 will show you the options available to you and how they may benefit you.

Table 18.1 The Sheet Tab Options

Option	Description
Print titles	You may have a large worksheet that includes column or row headings that you would like to see printed at the top of each page of your printed worksheet, to assist others in following the data. With this option you can select the columns and/or rows you want repeated
Gridlines	You may have formatted your tables quite nicely and so you would not want gridlines printed. However, if you want to show the table the way you see it in Excel, you can turn on gridlines
Comments	You learned how to insert comments earlier, but the default is that comments do not print. You can choose to print them as they appear on the sheet (which may cover up some data) or on a separate sheet at the end of the printed worksheet
Black and white	Makes your colours more readable if printing to a black/white printer by using shades of grey
Draft quality	Will print cell contents without gridlines or graphics. Mostly for speeding up printing, especially on older printers (and inkjet printers)
Row and column headings	Prints letters and numbers to make it easier to know which row and column your data is in
Cell errors as	You can determine whether you want cell errors to print as displayed, not at all, or in some other format
Page order	You can change the way your document prints. It can print down your spreadsheet, and then if the spreadsheet is longer it will cross over and print the pages from the top to the bottom on the left side. Or you can print it from left to right, allowing the spreadsheet to be printed in order

18

Timesaver tip

A quick way to print gridlines and headings is by selecting the Print checkbox next to each of these options located off the Sheet Options grouping on the Page Layout ribbon.

→ Printing Your Worksheet

Once you feel you have all your print setup completed you can move forward and actually print the worksheet. To do this, perform the following:

1 From within the worksheet you wish to print, select the Office Button.

2 Place your mouse over the Print option and then select the Print option that appears to the right.

3 The Print dialogue box will appear, as shown in Figure 18.9. Normally, the options presented are fine and you can hit OK. However, you may want to look over your options to make sure everything is correct, for example:

- *Printer Name*: Make sure this is the printer you want to print to. If you usually work with multiple printers, or a printer on your network, you may have to change this printer by selecting the down arrow and choosing another printer you have set up. If you don't see the printer you need, you should contact your network administrator (unless you know how to connect to printers on your own).

- *Print range*: You can print all the pages for your worksheet or you can determine you want to print only a selection. Note, if you want to print only one page (let's say page 3), you place a 3 in both the From and the To boxes.

- *Print what*: Lets you decide whether you want to print a selection that you have manually chosen, the active sheet (which is the default) or the entire workbook.

- *Copies*: You can print more than one copy. Specify the number of copies you want here. The Collate checkbox lets you print a complete copy of your print job before the next copy of your document will begin (valid only if you are printing multiple copies of your document).

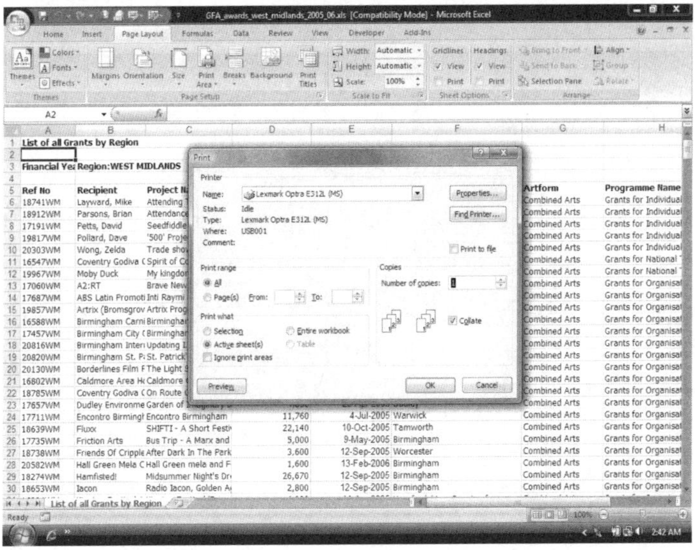

Figure 18.9
The Print dialogue box.

19

Sharing Your Documents

In this lesson you will learn how to share your documents with others without compromising personal data within the documents properties. You will also learn how to encrypt the document, mark a document as complete and more.

→ Prepare Options

One of the new features in Office 2007 is the ability to prepare your documents before you share them with others. In our modern world we constantly send documents to others: to our co-workers, to people in other companies, to people across the web whom we have no connection with ... we are a sharing generation.

From the Office Button, under the Prepare settings are a number of options, shown in Figure 19.1. We've considered some of these options in earlier chapters. In this chapter, we will consider only those portions of the Prepare settings that apply to sharing.

Figure 19.1
The Prepare options.

Document Properties

When you select the document Properties option from the Prepare settings you are given an added dialogue at the top of your workbook that allows you to enter personal information for others to see.

You can add some simple properties like the Author, Title, Subject and so forth. Or you can select the Document Properties down arrow to bring up a Properties dialogue box, which will allow you to add more to your documents properties and include additional categories. See Figure 19.2.

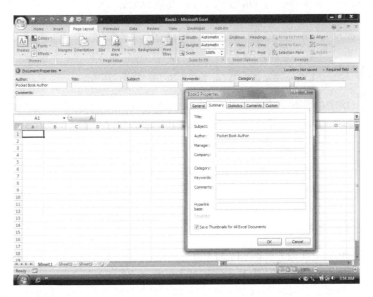

Figure 19.2
Document Properties.

Inspect Document

Although you may want to include certain properties in your documents, there are times when you need to prevent personal information from being sent out with your documents. Often you may not even be aware that these items are still included because they might be in the document properties, headers and footers, hidden text, comments and so forth.

19

To run the document inspector, perform the following:

1 Open the workbook you want to send to others.

2 Select the Office Button, place your mouse over the Prepare settings and then select Inspect Document. The Document Inspector dialogue appears, as shown in Figure 19.3.

3 If you select the Inspect button, it will scan through your document for metadata, revisions marks, etc. You can narrow down what you want inspected by de-selecting any of the checkboxes within the dialogue.

4 After the inspection you can choose "Remove All" to remove any of the data that it comes back as saying can pose a threat. Once the document has been cleared of all hidden data you can send it out without fear of private information being shared with others.

Jargon buster

Metadata has been defined as data that describes other data. This would include your document's properties.

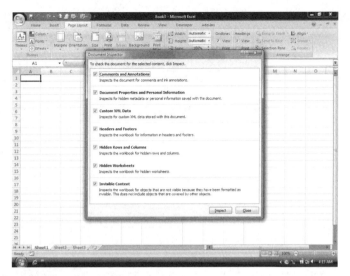

Figure 19.3
Using the Document Inspector to clean up your private data.

Encrypt Document

We discussed encryption in Chapter 13, but let's review this important feature involved in sharing your workbook. If you want to quickly encrypt your workbook before sending it out you can select the Office Button, under the Prepare settings, and select Encrypt Document.

You will see the Encrypt Document dialogue shown in Figure 19.4.

Mark as Final

When sharing a workbook with others you may want to take the added precaution of marking a workbook as read-only. This will prevent someone from altering the workbook.

To mark a workbook as read-only (aka mark as final) you can perform the following:

1 Open the workbook you want to make read-only.

2 Select the Office Button, place your mouse over the Prepare settings and then select **Mark as Final**. You will be prompted for approval and then the document will be marked.

19

Figure 19.4
Encrypting a document with a password.

3 There will be an icon in the status bar you will see because the document is marked as final.

4 To turn this feature off you return to the Prepare settings and de-select the option.

Run Compatibility Checker

Before sending out documents to others you may need to save the document in another format (for example, an *.xlsx document under the 2007 file type might need to be saved as an *.xls document for 97-2003 backward compatibility).

Before you save a document in another format it would be wise to check to see whether some items will no longer function properly within your workbook. To do this, select the **Run Compatibility Checker** from the Prepare options and your results will be displayed to you with any concerns regarding your compatibility, as shown in Figure 19.5.

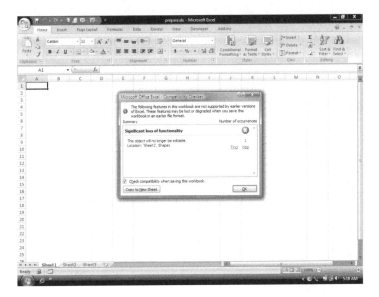

Figure 19.5
The Compatibility Checker flags concerns regarding your compatibility.

19

20

Proofing, Excel Options and Help

In this lesson you will learn how to use Excel's proofing and research tools, including Spell-check, Research, Thesaurus and Translate. In addition, you will 'look under the hood', so to speak and see all the options that you can alter for Excel to make it work the way you want it to.

→ Proofing Tools

We have covered just about every other tool that Excel 2007 has to offer, here are a few that may come in handy: Spelling, Research, Thesaurus and Translate.

Spell-check

Selecting the Spelling button (located under the Proofing grouping on the Review ribbon), as shown in Figure 20.1, will do a spell-check for your currently selected sheet.

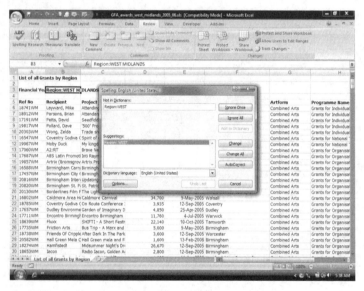

Figure 20.1
Performing a spell-check of your worksheet.

Research and Thesaurus

Selecting the Research button (located under the Proofing grouping on the Review ribbon), as shown in Figure 20.2, will open a side Research pane that allows you to type in searches for information that will be presented back to you either through a dictionary, an encyclopedia or some other reference work from the database of options. The thesaurus is one of those reference options that you can search for information in.

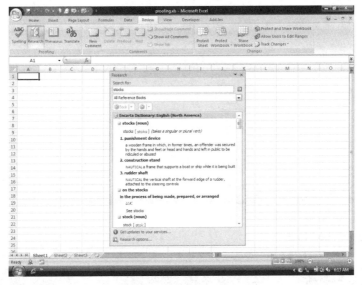

Figure 20.2
Using the Research options.

Translate

Another feature in Excel 2007 is the translation tool (located under the Proofing grouping on the Review ribbon), as shown in Figure 20.3. This is an invaluable tool to use when you are developing Excel worksheets and charts that may require you to use other languages. By researching a few words you can make your presentation stand out to readers who speak that language as their primary language.

20

Figure 20.3
Translation tools.

→ Excel Options

There are times when you may need to make some adjustments within your Excel application (some superficial in nature, others a bit deeper) and you will be referred to your Excel Options. It is not the intention of this chapter to explain each setting within those options. Rather, the intention is to show you the five primary screens so that you will have a better understanding of these options for the future.

To access the Excel Options, select the Office Button and then notice the Excel Options button next to the Exit Excel button. Select this option. There are more than five categories, but the top five include the following:

■ Popular

■ Formulas

- Proofing

- Save

- Advanced

Popular

The first category, the Popular category, shown in Figure 20.4, offers you many of the options you may have been wondering about all along.

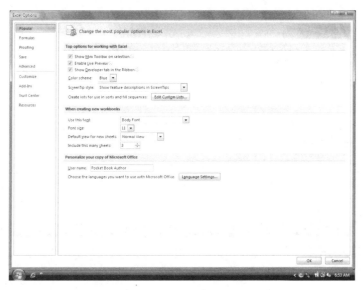

Figure 20.4
Excel Options: the Popular category.

For example, have you been wondering about the following questions?

- What if I want to start my workbooks with more than three sheets?

- What if I want to begin my view on Page Layout View?

- How do I turn off the mini-toolbar, it gets in my way?

- I've seen some of my friends have a silver look to their Excel, why is mine blue? How do I change that?

20

All of these options, and more, can be found under the Popular category of Excel Options.

Formulas

The second category, Formulas, shown in Figure 20.5, allows you to change options related to formula calculation, performance and error handling.

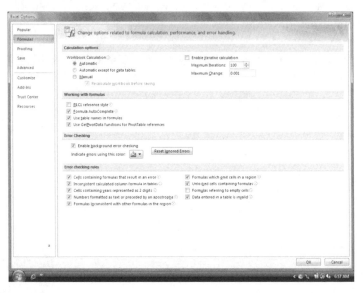

Figure 20.5
Excel Options: the Formulas category.

Important

For any of these features that you don't understand just yet, if you notice a small ⓘ (i with a circle), this is meant to provide you with information regarding that setting. Just place your cursor over the ⓘ and more information will appear.

Proofing

The third category, Proofing, shown in Figure 20.6, allows you to change options related to how Excel corrects and formats your text. These options do not just apply to Excel but to all your Office applications that use the same proofing tools.

Figure 20.6
Excel Options: the Proofing category.

The AutoCorrect options, shown in Figure 20.7, can be accessed to help you add new words, or eliminate those you don't need any longer.

Save

The fourth category, Save, shown in Figure 20.8, allows you to change options related to how Excel saves your workbooks. Some of the interesting options you can change here include the file format Excel uses by default, the AutoRecover options, the default location of files saved and more.

20

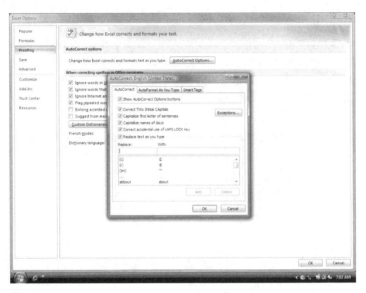

Figure 20.7
Excel Options: the Proofing category (AutoCorrect Options).

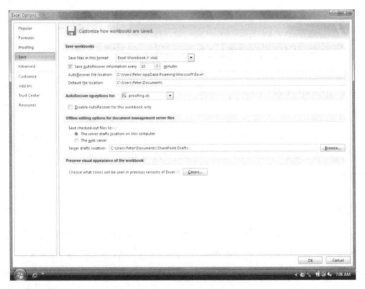

Figure 20.8
Excel Options: the Save category.

Advanced

The fifth category, Advanced, shown in Figure 20.9, pretty much covers all the other settings you might imagine under this one heading.

Figure 20.9
Excel Options: the Advanced category.

These settings include editing options, display settings for both your workbooks and your worksheets, and even the option to determine how multiple processor systems might be used to calculate formulas.

The Additional Settings

Within the Excel options you have four more categories to choose from, as follows:

■ *Customize*: For working with the Quick Access Toolbar (we worked on this one in Chapter 1).

■ *Add-Ins*: To view and manage Excel add-ins.

20

■ *Trust Center*: These options relate to keeping our documents safe and our computer secure and healthy.

■ *Resources*: Allows us to check for updates, run diagnostics, contact Microsoft, activate our Microsoft Office and/or learn more about the version of Office we are running.

→ Help Tools

For anyone reading this book who has worked in previous versions of Office and remembers the animated icons that tried to "help" us from time to time, you will be happy to know that the help structure for Office 2007 has been completely revamped.

In Excel 2007, to get help you have to ask for it (it doesn't just pop up whenever it feels you need it). You simply select the little white question mark in the blue circle in the top right-hand side of your Excel application. This will open up your Help menu, as shown in Figure 20.10.

Figure 20.10
The Help menu expanded to fill the screen.

You'll notice in the figure that there is a Table of Contents pane available which you can turn on and off. Enter text into the Search box to find the information you need. By default your search will look online in Microsoft's help database to get you the most up-to-date information. However, you can narrow your search to use only locally stored resources if you prefer. To view only locally stored help file information you select the down arrow next to the Search options and choose the Excel Help option located under the **Content from this computer** heading.

Timesaver tip

To get to your Help screen quicker, you simply have to press the F1 button.

→ Excel 2007: The Journey is Just Beginning

If you have gained an appreciation for one thing over these past 20 chapters, hopefully it is this: Excel 2007, as powerful a tool as it is, is not so complicated as to be beyond your ability to master. These lessons have begun the journey towards working with Microsoft's premier spreadsheet application. It is our hope that you will continue to progress in your knowledge of Excel.

A Chinese proverb says: "To get through the hardest journey we need take only one step at a time, but we must keep on stepping."

20